KU-360-538

SAMUEL SELVON

ELDORADO WEST ONE

PEEPAL   TREE

First published in Great Britain in 1988
Reprinted in 2008
Peepal Tree Press Ltd
17 King's Avenue
Leeds LS6 1QS
UK

501200350

© 1988, 2008 Samuel Selvon
Introduction © Susheila Nasta, 1988, 2008

ISBN: 0 94883 06 8
ISBN13: 978 0948833069

All rights reserved
No part of this publication may be
reproduced or transmitted in any form
without permission

ARTS COUNCIL ENGLAND   Peepal Tree gratefully acknowledges Arts Council support

CONTENTS

INTRODUCTION

Samuel Selvon was born in Trinidad in 1923 and is perhaps best known for his ten novels set both in the Caribbean and in London and his collection of short stories *Ways of Sunlight* (1958). Selvon, like many other young writers of his generation, migrated to the 'metropolis' of London in 1950; it was also the period when over 40,000 West Indians emigrated to Britain in search of employment after the Second World War. Selvon, unlike his fellow Trinidadian and contemporary, V. S. Naipaul, did not arrive in Britain with the notion that he could survive by his writing. He came like many others with the idea of finding employment and survived in the city by undertaking various part-time jobs and working as a freelance writer. It was only after the international recognition of his first novel *A Brighter Sun* (1952) and the appearance of his stories and reviews in a number of British newspapers and magazines that Selvon took the decision to become a professional writer. After the publication of An *Island is a World* (his second novel) in 1955 which coincided with a Guggenheim Fellowship, Selvon decided to devote himself to writing full-time. In his lifetime, Selvon was one of the Caribbean's most popular and internationally distinguished writers; his death in 1994 was greeted with an outpouring of sadness and affection.

While critical attention has frequently focused on Selvon's fiction, little mention has been made of either his contribution to Caribbean Drama or to his exploration of the Black British experience in his plays originally scripted for BBC Radio. From the late 1950s, Selvon was a regular writer for the BBC in London and until 1978, when he left Britain for Canada, over twenty of his plays were broadcast. Selvon was no novice with this form of writing; apart from the plays used by the BBC he was also responsible for writing

7

a screenplay for *The Lonely Londoners* (1956) which was commissioned by Robert Parish Enterprises in 1958 and was co-author, along with the director Horace Ove, of the film about West Indian immigrants in London entitled *Pressure.* The film was first released for public viewing in 1978 and was one of the first black feature films to be made in Britain. Some of Selvon's plays have been performed in Trinidad and Canada but it is only the stage play *Switch* (performed at the Royal Court Theatre in 1977) that has reached public attention in Britain. Describing his use of drama as a literary form, Selvon has said that his preference lies with the writing of plays for radio:

> I think drama for radio is much more imaginative and less limited than writing for stage... I like writing for radio because there is no limit to where one can place characters.

Selvon also liked the medium as it was a natural means by which he could examine further and elaborate on some of the central preoccupations of his art but in an alternative mode. Selvon's plays, like much of his fiction, revolve around the two central settings of Trinidad and London. The reader familiar with the range of Selvon's writing will immediately recognise developments amongst the plays of incidents and scenes familiar from novels and short stories as well as some interesting modifications.

Eldorado West One as the title suggests is a comic attempt to subvert and demythologise the colonial dream of the streets of London being 'paved with gold'. Characteristically, Selvon's reversal of the original myth (linked to the European voyages of discovery in the sixteenth and seventeenth centuries), of the possibility of inhabiting a land of gold and plenty has several important reverberations as far as the economic base of nineteenth century imperialism and Caribbean colonial history are concerned. The El Dorado of Selvon's black immigrants, however, is not gold but grey; his questers are limited to the bleak reality and emptiness of surviving in an alien and alienating 'mother-country.' The boundaries of Selvon's Black London are carefully defined and new arrivals require initiation into the rites of survival in a land where even amongst countrymen 'you don't know who is your friend and who is your enemy.' This shadowy world is bounded on the West by 'the Gate' (Notting Hill), on the East by 'the

8

Arch' (Marble) and in the North by 'the Water' (Bayswater).

As in the London novels, *The Lonely Londoners* (1956), *The Housing Lark* (1965), *Moses Ascending* (1975) and to some degree *Moses Migrating* (1983), Selvon's aim is to explore the experience of exile through the cultural displacement and confusion of a group of unlettered and mainly male West Indian immigrants as they attempt to colonise England in reverse, by the creation of a black enclave ('island') in the city. This sequence of seven short one act plays was written in 1969, in between the publication of Selvon's first novel of exile, *The Lonely Londoners,* and its sequel, *Moses Ascending.* Interestingly, several of the characters from both of these novels appear and a number of scenes from *The Lonely Londoners* are dramatised. The thematic focus on rooms as a metaphor for existence in this world also relates closely to all of Selvon's London novels. In addition, the dominant thread of the Moses story in these plays – his dream of return to Trinidad – is explored fully in Selvon's most recent novel, *Moses Migrating,* in which Moses finally returns across the Middle Passage as a black ambassador for Britain.

In the plays we have Moses, of course, who is reminiscing and recounting the story of his past experiences to the Black British reporter who is interviewing him (for a fee) and who represents a later generation of Blacks in Britain. Sir Galahad (alias Henry Oliver) is cast as the calypsonian trickster figure whose wheelings and dealings have far more serious implications when directed at his own community, a community which is fighting to live. Cap, the Nigerian, Tolroy, Tanty, Big City, Harris and many of the other 'boys' are also present, as well as some new characters such as Mr. Joseph, the parasitical white shopkeeper, who is lining his pockets with the effects that this immigration has produced. Bob, the white Man Friday from *Moses Ascending*, is also included but in quite a different role from the one he plays in that novel. In *Eldorado West One,* Bob is Moses's only true friend; it is only ever Bob, a white man, who actually does anything to improve Moses's predicament when he gives Moses his room upstairs (rather than in the base- ment) and finds him a job to help him earn his passage home. It is also Bob who constantly warns Moses to beware of the vulture-like mentality of the others towards his money or his time. In *Moses Ascending,* Bob, like Galahad, is a parasitical character and is out to exploit Moses's goodwill.

Several parallels exist between the actual content of *Eldorado West One* and *The Lonely Londoners* although there is considerable rearrangement of the sequence of material and the scenes selected for dramatisation. The opening of *Eldorado West One,* for instance, focuses on a scene in Moses's room where the boys congregate regularly to release their various woes. Moses makes the general theme clear from the outset. Referring to the stories of hardship he has heard repeatedly over the years he says: 'Got to pretend I sleeping, that's the only escape from the same old story, day after day'. The sense of stasis expressed by Moses here – a stasis which reflects a lack of movement or the potential for growth whatever the current 'ballad' or story – is central to Selvon's dramatic intention. In the novel, this scene in Moses's room forms one of the climactic moments towards its close and emphasises the fact that after all these years in Britain nobody has really moved; there is no coherence and there is no beginning or end to the experience. In the plays Selvon uses this scene to begin his dramatisation and interestingly combines it with Galahad's arrival at Waterloo, the opening scene of *The Lonely Londoners.* The juxtaposition of these two episodes, which are paralleled by Moses's own desperate dream of return, encapsulate an essentially linear plot or purpose. In a sense, a conventionally linear plot or development of action is irrelevant; the characters in these plays, as in the London novels, are caught in a circularity and transitoriness that can only be formally expressed by the fragmentary and episodic sequences of the drama. Furthermore it is drama itself which provides the means of defence in such a world, as one of V.S. Naipaul's characters once put it in *The Mimic Men,* 'From playacting to disorder; it is the pattern.' Whilst Selvon's characters may survive the demythologised metropolis in *Eldorado West One,* their only real defences are a melodramatic immersion in the comic and the creation of a superficially sustaining but ultimately undermining series of myths, dreams, ballads and self-caricatures.

Selvon's subject matter in *Eldorado West One* is, therefore, inherently dramatic and he exploits the potentiality of his characters and the language that they speak. The language world which these characters inhabit (rather like their two-dimensional names) establishes a corporate West Indian identity in the face of an alien and rejecting metropolis. The almost private language code used by the boys in their bantering, their anecdotes, their nicknames etc., makes the city seem intimate and recognisable. However, despite Tanty's attempts to even change the local shops, the common core rhetoric only creates a city of words and one which is as easily undermined as it is extended. The orality of Selvon's language form is fitting to the largely illiterate characters he portrays and represents (as did his use of 'dialect' in *The Lonely Londoners*), a modified form of Trinidadian speech patterns; it is a consciously chosen and deliberately modified use of Caribbean speech patterns that reflects the intonations and innuendoes of the tragi-comic humour. It is a form, as Selvon himself has pointed out, that lends itself to the 'dramatic' and the 'comic'; however, such comedy is often only a means of protection against the 'sufferings' and 'tribulations' his black immigrants have to undergo once the myth of the metropolis has been subverted and the realities of unemployment, poverty, poor accommodation and racism have been encountered.

In fact the nature of the underlying realism in some of the episodes in *Eldorado West One* is extremely disturbing. In 'Cap Captures a Bird', Selvon has developed and extended a humorous scene from *The Lonely Londoners* and exposed the almost tragic proportions of the poverty affecting figures like Cap who has no money or food. In addition the landlady's concern for the poor sea gull only adds to our sense of incongruity as Cap starves away and hides from her for fear of being evicted. Similarly in Tanty Has a Housing Problem', Selvon has incorporated new material which highlights the gravity of Galahad's trickery. Galahad is saving his own skin by attempting to evict Tolroy and family on behalf of Mr. Joseph, who is also a figure of corruption. However, Tanty's and Ma's honesty (they are representatives of the old folk morality of Jamaica where people's words to each other are kept) contrasts with the 'dog eat dog' mentality that surrounds them. Moses as a result loses more money and Tanty and Tolroy almost lose their house. The comedy in many senses is much more threatening than that in *The Lonely Londoners*. Mr. Joseph ultimately feeds off Galahad by oppressing him; later he attempts to exploit and patronise Tanty by using her as a marketing 'piece' to sell more goods in his shop. The money Tanty raises to pay Moses's passage back home and to ease her conscience is only obtainable through Mr. Joseph's exploitation and stems from conning an American tourist into buying a chair, the only authentic possession Moses has to symbolise his experiences with the boys in Britain. And it is money that comes from *outside* the community.

In *Eldorado West One,* Selvon's immigrants are not allowed the luxury of a home or house and all that that implies. Their constant instability is symbolised by their fragmented room-based existence, a fragmentation which reflects their economic predicament and the impossibility of securing any stable base for existence. The absence of long term sexual relationships – love, marriage – and the preponderance of rootless, male characters is another aspect of this. Selvon has developed the roles of several female figures in these plays; we have extended scenes between Tanty, Ma and Tolroy; also the inclusion of Daisy and Bob's girlfriend, but women nevertheless remain depicted as objects either of scorn or sexual possession. The sexism in the depiction of women in the plays is not just a simple chauvinism but the mirroring and objectification of the extent to which the male characters are also regarded as 'objects' by the wider British society. This is not to excuse the sexism but to point perhaps to the extent to which Galahad's desire to possess the 'white pussy', Daisy, is a reflection of his own unease.

This collection of Selvon plays has not been available previously because they were originally written as scripts for radio. It is hoped that teachers who wish to use this material for drama in the classroom will welcome this resource. They could be used either as independent units with broad scope for improvisation or as a complimentary text to *The Lonely Londoners.* Certainly the plays will raise a number of important points for discussion such as the difference between the Britain of Selvon's Moses and the Black British experience today. Creative writing could also be encouraged either in the form of developing themes into stories or through script writing. Students could also attempt to conduct their own research and interviews with parents and friends who lived in Britain during this period. These types of projects could be written up in a variety of styles and forms.

Susheila Nasta

CHARACTERS

MOSES ALOETTA: Moses is a Trinidadian whose basement flat is the meeting place for the boys. Moses affects a cynical exterior but is inevitably too trusting for his own good. His overriding ambition is to go back home to Trinidad.

REPORTER: A young Black Briton, he shares the 'present' with Moses whom he is interviewing as one of the first generation of arrivants.

GALAHAD: Sir Galahad, Henry Oliver, another Trinidadian, is a calypsonian trickster figure. There is almost nothing he wouldn't stoop to if it was to his advantage.

DAISY: Sir Galahad's white girlfriend; she wants fun but is reluctant to allow Galahad to claim absolute possession over her.

BART: A light-skinned Trinidadian who tries to make his passage easier by claiming to be a Latin American.

BIG CITY: An 'illegal' immigrant who jumped ship and is hooked by the bright lights of Londontown.

CAP: A Nigerian Prince, or so he tells his friends. He exists on a very occasional allowance from home and whatever he can persuade his acquaintances to part with. He has a certain easy-come, easy-go charm which attracts Daisy, whom he would like to take from under Galahad's nose.

MRS. WATSON: Cap's reluctant landlady.

BOB: A white worker at Moses's factory who is his only true friend.

MAUREEN: Bob's girlfriend, and later his wife.

TOLROY: A Jamaican, one of the boys until his mother, aunt and other members of his family arrive.

MA: Tolroy's mother, who brings her integrity and her hard work with her.

TANTY: Tolroy's aunt. She sees no reason why she should change, carrying out a one woman campaign to get the local shopkeepers to adapt to West Indian ways. Though she's getting older, she sees no reason why she shouldn't enjoy life. Tanty comes from a world where neighbours are to be trusted and she discovers that this is a dangerous assumption in London.

HARRIS: Harris sees himself as a small-time entrepreneur and community leader. He is a 'Black Englishman', always proper and embarrassed by the 'vulgarity' of his fellow West Indians.

MR. JOSEPH: A white shopkeeper and slum landlord who battens on the needs of the West Indian community.

REPORTER: A white reporter, ignorant of the Caribbean and naively offensive in the assumptions he makes.

AMERICAN: A gullible American tourist whose avidity for bits of Old England finally helps Moses achieve his goal.

SPEAKER: A Black Power orator at Hyde Park Corner.

HOUSEHOLDER: A working-class white male.

PORTER: A white worker.

TICKET COLLECTOR: A white worker.

SHOPPERS, CROWD VOICES: Mainly West Indian.

PART ONE: ELDORADO WEST ONE

REPORTER: [*Young Black Briton*] Moses, you were one of the first West Indians to come to Britain, and now you're planning to go back to Trinidad. Can you tell me something about your early days in Britain in the fifties?

MOSES: Well, that's a story, ain't it? But it's a long one. You too young to remember the old days.

REPORTER: Try me.

MOSES: Well in them days people from the Caribbean land up here believing what the newspapers tell them.

REPORTER: What's that?

MOSES: That the streets of London paved with gold.

REPORTER: Ah! A sort of Eldorado West One.

MOSES: Something like that.

REPORTER: Well, let's call it that... We present Eldorado West One... etc. etc.

MOSES: You making me throw my mind far back... to them Sunday mornings when the boys used to congregate in the dingy basement room I had in Bayswater...

... Moses is in his bed in the basement. He can hear the voices of his visitors, Cap, Big City and Bart, approaching...

Lord... these boys here once again and I just come off Saturday night-shift in that factory... Praise be, this going to be my last year in the old Brit'n... this blooming basement with the skylight leaking for the fog to come through... and this dilapidated bed what that Polish landlord frighten to change... but just let them wait, I make up my mind definitely this year... is back home to Trinidad away from all this... just listen to the idleness they talking... I got to pretend I sleeping, that's the only escape from the same old story, day after day...

15

BART: …so he ask me where I come from, and I tell him the Latin American countries.

BIG CITY: Bart, why you like to lie so? Just because you light skin? Everybody know you come from the backwoods of Trinidad.

BART: I not like you, Big City, I didn't desert no ship when I see the bright lights of Londontown. I come to this country legally. And in truth and in fact, my mother had Spanish blood. You could ask Cap.

CAP: I don't know about you, Bart, but my father was a chieftain in Nigeria.

BIG CITY: [*Talking like a Nigerian*] I know, bo, is how you ah- go, oh?

CAP: [*In good humour*] I go so-so, bo, you know, oh?

BART: What I find hard to accept is how the English group me with you fellars who have roots in Africa...

There is general laughter at this, during which the door opens and Harris enters, with brolly and bowler, more English than the English.

HARRIS: [*Shivering*] It's terribly foggy out... You boys sit down here in this cold basement room? None of you have a shilling for the gas?

BIG CITY: If you stick me with a pin you wouldn't draw blood.

BART: I glad you come, Harris. I wanted to ask you to lend me ten bob until next week, please God.

HARRIS: [*Ignoring this completely, sighing*] I suppose I'll have to put one in... [*Moves towards fire*] ... shift your foot, Cap... [*He puts a coin in the meter and lights the fire... There are murmurs of appreciation*]

CAP: Ah! We might be able to raise a cup of tea now.

HARRIS: [*Concerned*] Bart, you didn't wake up Moses, and you know he has to go to Waterloo to meet the boat-train?

BART: He only playing possum, he ain't sleeping in truth!

HARRIS: [*Shaking Moses*] Moses! Time to get up, boy!

There is a grunt from Moses as he turns over and covers himself.

BIG CITY: Leave him, Harris, he just come off night-shift... Fill up the kettle and put on the gas-ring, somebody.

HARRIS: [*As somebody does that*] Move up on the edge of the bed, Big City, we not in the Waldorf.

CAP: See what Moses have in the cupboard as you on your feet, Harris.

MOSES: [*Leaping up in bed, flinging the blankets aside*] Leave my bloody cupboard alone! I giving you all board and lodging in Bayswater? Every Sunday morning is the same blasted thing. The whole set of you coming round here, burning my gas and eating my rations. What you-all going to do when I go? What you-all going to do when I take off for Trinidad like a bullet?

There is a kind of repressed tittering and spluttering of lips

CAP: [*Very innocently*] You really going back home?

BART: You been singing that for years.

MOSES: [*Vehemently, in a low voice*] Wait. Just wait. Boy, I will be sitting down on the beach in Maracas Bay drinking fish-tea and digging up the yampee between my toes, thinking about all you bastards suffering in the old Brit'n. Just wait and see.

BIG CITY: If you go back home you will be like Cap, the wandering Nigerian, owing people rent all over London.

MOSES: Go on, laugh. Laugh your belly full... Harris, look up there on the mantelpiece, you will see some papers. See if is joke I making this time.

HARRIS: What papers, Moses? These advertisements? It says here that the *Hildebrand* sailing for the Caribbean next week... and the week after there's a Booker's boat stopping at Jamaica on the way to B.G.

MOSES: That's the one. I never seen that raas-Jamaica yet, is only in Brit'n I ever meet Jamaicans. And seeing as they always call me 'Jamaican', I might as well see what it like.

BART: Ahh, them is only ads, man. Anybody could walk in any travel agency and get them. Who you trying to fool? You put down deposit?

BIG CITY: Yes, that's the thing. You book? Last year you make the same grand-charge.

CAP: [*Chuckling*] And the year before that.

MOSES: [*Settling back on the bed*] Go on, don't mind me. But you know the old saying, 'You never miss the water till the well runs dry.'

CAP: You know you not going no place, man! You have some bread? If it stale we could toast it by the gas fire.

HARRIS: You chaps! I really have to agree with Moses, you know. One would think you were starving in this country.

17

BIG CITY: We ain't far from it... But Moses, you promise to help me check this football coupon. I sure I hit them this week. And then you know what? You know what when I hit a first dividend?

BART: What?

BIG CITY: I only buying out a whole set of rooms in the Water, and I only letting out rooms to the boys, and I putting a notice in the window, 'Sorry, no Whites.' With proper spelling, too.

HARRIS: Why don't you chaps go out and leave Moses in peace?

CAP: Listen to you, Harris. I suppose you collect big from that dance you had in Willesden last night? I see you putting a shilling in the gas. When is the next fete?

HARRIS: Well... I've been thinking, maybe in the summer. I want to have a real big do at St. Pancras Town Hall. But you chaps must bring some good manners along... Ah... Moses getting up!

MOSES: [*Getting out of bed now*] Out! Every manjack out! This room ain't Hyde Park Corner to congregate and disturb the peace.

BART: You not getting on catholic this morning.

MOSES: I have to go out. Give me some elbow room to get dress.

CAP: You putting we out in the cold? It ain't spring yet.

HARRIS: Actually, spring isn't far away. I'm sure I heard the first cuckoo in the park this morning. I must write to the *Times*.

MOSES: [*He is pushing them out now*] I say out, man. You all want me to spell it?

BART: [*Reluctant*] If that's the mood you in... What time you coming back from Waterloo?

BIG CITY: And what happen to you, Harris. You didn't hear the man say out?

HARRIS: [*Helping Moses to push them out*] I have some private business to discuss with Moses... Come on... Come on... [*He closes the door as they leave, and sighs*] Honestly! These boys! I don't know what to say for them. They behave just as if they were back home in the islands.

MOSES: [*Sitting on the bed*] Pass them shoes for me, there, near the chair... [*The kettle whistles*] And you might as well make a cup. No use wasting hot water.

HARRIS: [*Turning the gas-ring off*] You have any sugar?

MOSES: Look in the cupboard... hurry up, man, just put the tea in the cups and pour the water in.

HARRIS: [*Stirring the tea*] What time you have to be there?

18

MOSES: You know these boat-trains... they always late... Pass that comb and brush off the mantelpiece for me... and drink your tea quick.

HARRIS: [*Sipping tea*] I am lunching with Lord Ullin today.

MOSES: Good for you. I would of offered you some sardine and bread, but if that's the case...

HARRIS: [*Quickly*] I wouldn't object to a little aperitif... Actually I'm not sure... I have to phone and confirm.

MOSES: We ain't have time anyway... You ready? Turn off the fire. Let's go.

Moses is walking the streets through a London fog on the way to Waterloo...

MOSES: This damn fog, a man can't even breath now... look at my handkerchief, black... Those reprobates and vagabonds! The same blasted thing week after week, boy Moses, help me out of this; boy Moses, help me out of that... But let them wait... [*Chuckle*] This year they going to be surprise... What London do to me that I still hustling around after ten years, as if English people have something to give me, as if one day the Queen going to call me to Buckingham Palace and make me Knight or O.B.E. or something!... Damn reprobates and scoundrels, the lot of them, always antsing on a man... I going to put a stop to all that... It would really give me kicks to sit down in the sun back home and think how Cap hustling for a place to live, or Bart get kick out of a pub because his skin not clear enough... But I better make the move soon, before moss start to grow on me in the old Brit'n... I won't like to be dead over here, it's a wonder a car ain't knock me down already, the way it have so much traffic. I mean, them drivers only have to see a spade crossing the road and all they have to do is step on the X and bam! One more spade bite the dust, no fuss, no bother, not even a quarter inch in a local paper... [*He gives a deep rattling cough*] Look at me going out in this weather to meet a man I don't even know, a friend of a friend... I really must put a stop to all this big-heart business... [*A long sigh*] I must ask this feller how things is in Trinidad, because really I can't face another winter... [*He chuckles*] Soon, boy, soon! And then I taking off like a kite...

Moses is in Waterloo Station. There is a confused milling mob of West Indians waiting for the boat-train. Moses is sitting on a bench when a Jamaican friend. Tolroy, comes up.

TOLROY: Aye, Moses. I didn't expect to meet you in Waterloo, for arrivals.

MOSES: The next time will be my departure, please God. The boat-train late.

TOLROY: Who you meeting.

MOSES: Some fellar name Henry.

TOLROY: Boy, I expecting my mother.

MOSES: All-you fellars really have guts, yes, Tolroy. Where you going to put she, in that two-be-four you have in the Harrow Road?

TOLROY: I have to look for a bigger place. You know any?

MOSES: Look, one of your Jamaican countrymen over there waiting like a hawk for tenants. He have a lot of houses in Brixton.

TOLROY: You know what that set-up like. A chair, a table, and he hitting you anything from three to five guineas.

MOSES: You try down by Ladbroke Grove? Since they kill Kelso, English people been evacuating like Dunkirk from that area. You *bound* to get a room.

TOLROY: Down there too grim.

MOSES: What you want, Belgravia? Park Lane? Maybe you could put she up at the Dorchester till you find a place...

The station loudspeaker announces the arrival of the boat-train. There is a hubbub as they all surge near the barrier. The train comes in. Moses and Tolroy stand to one side, out of the noisy greetings and general milling. An English newspaper reporter comes up to them.

REPORTER: [*English*] Excuse me sir, have you just arrived from Jamaica?

MOSES: Am... er, yes.

REPORTER: I'm from the *Echo*... Would you like to tell me what conditions there are like?

TOLROY: [*Enjoying the situation*] Yes, Moses, go on and tell him.

MOSES: Well, the situation is desperate as usual. You know that big hurricane it had a few weeks ago?

REPORTER: Yes?

MOSES: Well I was in that hurricane. You could ask my friend here if you think I lie. I was sitting down in my mansion when suddenly I look up and see the sky. What you think happen?

REPORTER: What?

MOSES: Hurricane blow the roof clean off, banana plantation lay down as if they gone asleep...

REPORTER: Tell me, sir, why are so many Jamaicans coming to England? It is now about thirteen years since the war. Do you believe the streets are paved with gold?

MOSES: I don't know about all of them, but sometimes in the night I see as if the Bayswater Road sparkling with diamonds. But then you look in truth you see is only stones and gravel that mix-up with the asphalt. You know of any London street what pave with gold?

REPORTER: Thank you for that statement. I'll just talk to a few others...

MOSES: [*Chuckling*] Watch him! Like he going to tackle that family what coming off the train.

TOLROY: [*In consternation*] Oh rarse! That look like my mother! And.... and, Tanty! And Agnes and Lewis!... and the two children! What the hell happening in Londontown today! [*He starts to elbow through the crowds, shouting*] Ma! Look me over here!... [*As he gets near them, panting*] What is this all?

MA: Tolroy boy! You don't remember your own mother?

TOLROY: [*In a daze*] But what Tanty doing here, Ma? And Agnes and Lewis and the children?

MA: All of we come, Tolroy. This is how it happen: when you write home to say you getting five pounds a week, Lewis say, 'Oh God, I going to England tomorrow'. Well Agnes say she not staying home alone with the children, so all of we came.

TOLROY: [*Weakly*] And Tanty?

MA: Well, you know how old your Tanty getting. Is a shame to leave she alone to dead in Kingston with nobody to look after she.

TOLROY: [*Utterly stunned*] Oh lord, oh lord, oh lord...

TANTY: [*Indignantly*] Tolroy! You not going to kiss me? Your own Tanty?

MA: Give him a chance, Tanty, he didn't expect all of we...

TANTY: You see what I tell you. He still ungrateful! I would go back

21

to Kingston on this selfsame train. He don't remember when he used to live by me and I uses to send him to school and give him tea and bake in the evening. He don't remember when I give him shoes to wear and pants to put on his backside.

TOLROY: [*Moaning*] You don't know what you put yourself in...

PORTER: [*Trying to pass by*] Come on there, out of the way...

TANTY: Look at trouble here! Mister, you hads best mind what you doing. If you touch me I call a policemen for you...

MA: [*In awed tone*] Keep quiet, Tanty! You can't see him white?

REPORTER: [*Coming up*] Excuse me, I'm from the *Echo*. Is this your first trip to England?

TOLROY: [*Growling*] Don't tell that man nothing.

TANTY: Why you so prejudice? The gentleman ask me a good question, why shouldn't I answer? [*To reporter*] Yes, mister, is my first trip.

REPORTER: Have you any relatives here? Are you going to live in London?

TANTY: Well my nephew Tolroy here in this country a long time, and so he send for the rest of the family to come and live with him. Not so Tolroy?

TOLROY: [*Overwhelmed*] I going to help Lewis with the luggage.

REPORTER: Just one more question, madam. Can you tell me why so many people are leaving Jamaica and coming to England? Isn't it a bit far from home at your age?

TANTY: [*Warming up*] Is the same thing I say! I tell all of them who coming, 'Why all-you leaving the country to go to England? Over there so cold that only white people live there.' But they say it have work in England, and better pay...

MA: [*Interrupting, in cautious tone*] You best stop talking as Tolroy say...

TANTY: What happening to you? You can't see this white gentleman from the newspapers come to meet we at the station? We have to show that we have good manners, you know.

REPORTER: I'd like to take a picture, if I may.

TANTY [*To Ma*] There! You see? He wants to take photo. Where all the children [*Shouts*] Tolroy! Agnes! Lewis! All-you come to take photo, children. The mister want a snapshot.

REPORTER: They're busy with the luggage... one of you will be all right.

TANTY: You can't take me alone, you have to take the whole family…
   [*Loudly*] Come on, children! We lucky! We just land up in
   England, a mister want to take photo! [*Low, to Ma*] Ma, open up
   the cardboard box and take out my straw hat for me… [*Sharply,
   to child*] Eloisa, straighten your dress!

REPORTER: [*Impatiently*] Are you ready now?

TANTY: Just a minute… Agnes, you stand up near Lewis, and put the
   children to stand in front… thank you, Ma. I bring this hat
   specially all the way.

REPORTER: Just hold it for a minute [*He takes two or three shots*]
   Thank you… that's fine. I hope you don't find our weather too
   cold for you…

TOLROY: [*Coming up, angry*] Come on and get all the blooming
   luggage. Don't bother with that man.

*The focus moves to Moses, who has been standing by as a quiet
onlooker. We hear him ruminating…*

MOSES: [*With a gentle chuckle*] You see what I mean about harking
   back to them good old days? Now they catching jet and landing
   in the airport in style… but in my time, men would paddle a
   canoe from Tobago to Plymouth… Look at poor Tolroy! … I
   remember when I did first come to Britain to do my little spot
   for the war, men never used to dream about living in this
   country. And watch how things turn out. Maybe Tanty think the
   cold might preserve she for a few more years – how a man could
   tell what people think? But like hell 'pon jackass back for Tolroy,
   as the saying goes. That two-be-four batch that he have could
   barely hold a single bed… I wonder how many Trinidadians
   come this time. I could only classify them like the English – all
   black. Is only in this country that I get to meet Barbadians, and
   Grenadians, and rarse-Jamaicans. I never bounce up with one of
   them specimen in Trinidad… Like the crowd thinning out and
   I can't see this Henry fellar. I stopping right here in this corner,
   and if he don't see me, that's his bad luck. I see it have some
   fellars here what carrying placards with their names written on
   it, so the people they come to meet could identify them. But I not
   so thirsty to meet this Henry… I wonder if that is him coming
   up from the last carriage? I better get out of this corner as he is
   passing…

Henry Oliver, known hereafter as Sir Galahad, dressed casually as if for the tropics, is strolling up the platform without a care in the world. He is the last passenger to detrain. He comes up to Moses.

GALAHAD: Ah, you must be Moses, from the description I get.

MOSES: I was almost hoping – I mean thinking, that you weren't coming again. You are the great Henry Oliver, eh?

GALAHAD: Yes man... [*Looks around*] So this is where I meet my Waterloo, eh? What is that thing over there?

MOSES: You not feeling cold? You didn't bring a coat?

GALAHAD: Is so the winter does be? It not so bad, In fact I feeling a little warm.

MOSES: [*Alarmed*] Oh lord, don't tell me you land-up sick?

GALAHAD: Who me? Sick? You must be making joke!

MOSES: You must have bags of wool under that tropical suit, then.

GALAHAD: No. I travel light.

MOSES: Where your luggage?

GALAHAD: Well I got a toothbrush...

MOSES: Now ain't time to make joke, man. We got to get away. Boy, I longing to drink a Trinidad rum, and to smoke an Anchor. They still have Anchor?

GALAHAD: I didn't bring anything in truth. As soon as I start to work I will get what I need.

MOSES: You mean you come all the way like that? You didn't see the letter I write Chapman? And Chapman himself know what Brit'n like?

GALAHAD: [*Coolly*] Oh you know how them fellars like to exaggerate.

MOSES: [*Groaning*] Disaster...

GALAHAD: Take it easy, man, don't panic. I will get fix up as soon as I get a work.

MOSES: You does smoke?

GALAHAD: Yes thanks. I finish my last pack on the train. Boy, is a long trip from the seaside! This country must be really big, eh? But I will soon get my bearings.

MOSES: You don't know they does allow you to land with two hundred cigarettes? And what about rum? Two whole bottles you could have brought. You know how much it cost here?

GALAHAD: How much?

MOSES: Thirty-seven and six.

GALAHAD: How much that is in Trinidad money?

MOSES: Only about ten dollars... [*Henry whistles*] I suppose you bring some money, though?

GALAHAD: I have three pounds. Actually it was five, but the boys was playing some *wapee* on board...

MOSES: [*Resignedly*] All right, Sir Galahad, take it easy. London will do for you before long... We better catch a tube to Bayswater...

In the tube station.

GALAHAD: [*Man of the world attitude*] I know about these trains what does run under the ground, Moses. And the escalators-them. Is people like Tolroy family you got to worry about! Watch at Tanty over there!

TANTY: [*Loudly, as she approaches the escalator*] You want to kill me, Tolroy! I never see steps what moving before!

TOLROY: [*Exhausted with his troubles*] All the others gone down, Tanty, and nothing happen to them. Just step on slowly.

TANTY: I wouldn't go on that thing if they pay me!

TICKET COLLECTOR: Come on, you lot. You can't stand there all day.

TOLROY: You hear what the man say? Oh lord... [*He sees Moses*] Moses! Come help me get Tanty down here.

MOSES: [*Chuckling*] I got enough headache here with Sir Galahad.

GALAHAD: [*Pretending indifference*] Don't mind me, I... [*He steps on the escalator carelessly and slips... Moses roars with laughter*] What-the-hell!

MOSES: In London you have to keep on the move all the time, you see. Even the steps keep moving... Get up man, and just stand up like me...

TANTY: You see what happen to that fellar? I going to walk, Tolroy, just tell me which part this gracious Harrow Road is...

Moses and Galahad arrive in Bayswater. Moses opens the street door with his key.

GALAHAD: You got to go down to go up?

MOSES: No. I living in the basement.

GALAHAD: What! Under the ground again?

MOSES: [*Irritable with Galahad's cockiness*] Look, old man, before you

25

enter this basement you better understand one thing. I only helping you out because of Chapman, who ease me out of a difficult situation when he was in Brit'n. So cut down on all the remarks.

GALAHAD: [*Sulking*] I was only thinking that if you tell people in Trinidad that you living under the ground they might laugh at you.

MOSES: That is Trinidad. This is Brit'n. You best hads get that straight from now. Come on... [*They go in and Moses opens his door. They enter*] Sit down somewhere... not in the armchair, that's mine. Use the other one. Let we get something to eat.

GALAHAD: [*Sitting*] This is a small room, man. And like the wallpaper rebelling.

MOSES: [*Taking a pot of food from the cupboard*] Never mind. You will get a mansion for yourself... You have a shilling change on you?

GALAHAD: I think so... [*Hands Moses the coin*] What you want it for?

MOSES: The gas, man, the gas. It don't light unless you get money in the meter. Watch how I doing it... [*Puts coin in the meter*] ...And you best hads be careful to turn it off always when you going out, and when you sleeping.

GALAHAD: Else what?

MOSES: Else you dead... [*He lights the fire and puts a pot on the gas-ring*] Just let this peas and rice warm up a little. I hungry too bad... Boy, you mean to say you really didn't even bring a bottle of pepper sauce.

GALAHAD: Chapman had some things to send for you, but the man not reach when the boat was ready to leave. He say he will post them.

MOSES: [*Sighing*] Just my luck... Anyway, seeing as you ain't even bring a nip of rum to celebrate your coming to the Mother Country, you might as well start to learn the facts. What work you does?

GALAHAD: Carpentry.

MOSES: Skilled or unskilled?

GALAHAD: How you mean?

MOSES: You got any papers? You got any recommendations?

GALAHAD: Man, I prepare to do anything.

MOSES: Is as well. Because the only sort of work you going to get is donkey work. Make up your mind to lift heavy crates, or sweep the streets, or something.

26

GALAHAD: What you does do?

MOSES: I got a night-shift in a small factory what does make pot scourers... But first thing tomorrow, bright and early, you go and register at the labour exchange. And any work they offer you, you take it. Because you in a desperate situation, old man.

GALAHAD: Man must live!

MOSES: That slogan don't work over here... Look in the cupboard and pass two plate and two spoon.

GALAHAD: [*As he does this*] Work hard to get, then?

MOSES: [*Dishing out the food*] You will get all the gen at the exchange.

GALAHAD: [*Confidently*] Ah, you only trying to frighten me, Moses. Just because you been here a few years...

MOSES: Ten years... [*Suddenly brightening up*] and returning home soon! In all the confusion I almost forget I have that consolation.

GALAHAD: [*Eating*] You really going back?

MOSES: If I lie I die! How things going back home?

GALAHAD: Rough, boy, rough.

MOSES: Nothing could be rougher than Brit'n... Where you used to live?

GALAHAD: Down South, San Fernando.

MOSES: I know South well, man! You know Mahal, the mad Indian fellar who used to go around town playing as if he driving car, putting in gear and stepping on the X and making hand signals and blowing horn?

GALAHAD: How you mean? Everybody know Mahal?

MOSES: [*Chuckling*] He must be catching hell with the new type of gear it have on them cars now! And what about Palace Theatre? It still there? I remember the film always used to bust when they had a show.

GALAHAD: Yes, the Palace still there. But they only showing a set of Indian pictures now.

MOSES: What about the market? I hear they build it over... And Charley pudding! You know Charley pudding?

GALAHAD: He have a big shop down Broadway now.

MOSES: Boy, I remember that Chinaman used to make the best black pudding in Trinidad... He must be making a lot of money eh? ...And what about Skinner's Park?

GALAHAD: All those places and people still there, man.

MOSES: Even Mussolini? The one-foot fellar what used to sell newspapers by the Library Corner?

GALAHAD: No, he dead. A car knock him down in Coffee Street.

MOSES: [*Chuckling*] I remember one time Mussolini try to run after me and I trip him up... You should of hear him curse!

GALAHAD: Which part the Labour Exchange is?

MOSES: And what about up in Port of Spain? I had a aunt living in Laventille... You never see she?

GALAHAD: What about a place to live? I could stay here with you?

MOSES: Boy, when I go back home I going to look up all the old places and all the old friends I have... [*Stops abruptly as Galahad's words register*] What is that you say?

GALAHAD: I could stay here for the time being? I mean, being as both of we is Trinidadians together...

MOSES: [*Back to reality*] They don't have any of that crap here. You stay tonight – you have to make-do in the armchair. But start hustling tomorrow for a room.

GALAHAD: I have an address of a fellar in Brixton... that far from here?

MOSES: Anywhere from the Water is far for me.

GALAHAD: You mean Bayswater, where we is now?

MOSES: The Water. You will learn. The Arch is Marble Arch, the Grove is Ladbroke Grove... [*Belches loudly*] Ah, that was good. God bless for that meal. You sure you haven't any cigarettes? Maybe if you look in your breast pocket you might find a crumple-up pack that you forget.

GALAHAD: [*Searching*] I don't think so... aps! Like you right!

MOSES: What is it? Anchor?

GALAHAD: Anchor Special. And it only have two!

MOSES: Never mind, I grateful for small mercies. I will keep mine for later... You tired?

GALAHAD: Yes, man, all that travelling.

MOSES: Good. Because I going to sleep now. This nightwork killing me. Wash up them things in the sink, let me see if I have an old blanket to spare... [*Opening the cupboard*] I ain't got one... [*Grudgingly*] I suppose I could lend you mine for tonight until you buy one...

GALAHAD: How much?

MOSES: About three quid for a warm one... And you also got to get a coat, else cold kill you in this country.

GALAHAD: How much?

MOSES: Hmmm... Even a second-hand one in Edgeware Road would be about five quid... That make eight in all.

GALAHAD: I would pay you back, Moses, as soon as I start to work...

MOSES: Pay me back! You think I going to break in that money what I been saving for my passage back home?

GALAHAD: I pay you back, Moses, first thing... A couple of weeks or so can't make all that difference. Have some compassion for a fellow countryman!

MOSES: Don't hand me none of that! You asking me to put off this trip what I been trying to make for years?

GALAHAD: Just a few weeks, Moses! Trinidad won't sink in the sea in that time! I tell you what – I will even give you a little bonus a little bonus on top of that eight pounds. I will give you ten instead... [As Moses hesitates] Please man.

MOSES: My soft heart always making me lose out in the long run...

GALAHAD: And then Spring is just round the corner! I mean you not going to quit Brit'n now when the birds start to sing and the daffodils start to bloom, and all them English girls I hear about walking around without no winter coats to hide the legs?

MOSES: You got a point there...

GALAHAD: Matters settle, then... You don't have to worry about me, I will just curl up in the armchair...

MOSES: [Sitting on the bed] Yes... with my blanket... Anyway, you comfortable enough?

GALAHAD: [Yawning, going to sleep] Yes... I so tired I could... sleep anywhere...

MOSES: [Stretching out on the bed] Now for my Anchor... [Strikes a match, lights the cigarette, inhales deeply and exhales with a contented sigh] Ah... Is a pity you don't know my aunt up Laventille. You sure? She have a little parlour selling rock and mauby.

GALAHAD: [Sleepily] I don't know Laventille well.

MOSES: I might have to go and stay by she for a few days when I land... They still have horse-racing Christmas time?

GALAHAD: [Almost asleep] Ah-ha.

MOSES: I used to like that. But I never been in this country... Another thing is the football pools. That start up in Trinidad yet?... [Galahad starts to snore] ...well at least you spending your first night in Brit'n with a roof over your head!... Hmmmn, is a funny thing how you come when I just getting ready to go... As soon as you pay me back, you going to be on your own, Mister Galahad, freezing and shivering, looking for a place to live. And this time so, old Moses back home in the sun, sitting down on a sandy beach, only laughing at fellars like you and Cap, and Bart and Big City... and don't forget Tolroy! [*He chuckles*] Lord! I could imagine the pandemonium and the panic, the disaster and the catastrophe that going on in Harrow Road with the set of them... boy Galahad, I pray the Lord you get a work quick and pay me that ten pounds... and then... [*Luxurious yawn as he falls asleep*] I will be out of all this confusion, basking under a coconut tree...

PART TWO: MOSES GEARS FOR THE TROPICS

REPORTER: [*Black Briton*] Now, Moses, surely it didn't take Galahad all this time to pay you back the money he borrowed?

MOSES: Oh no. I soon got him fixed up in the factory where I work.

REPORTER: So, Moses, tell me why it's taken you so long to leave?

MOSES: I going to tell you what happen if you give me a chance.

REPORTER: Of course. That's why we're here... I wonder what happened to those poor old ladies?

MOSES: You mean Tanty and Ma?

REPORTER: That's right! They must have had a hard time settling down? Did Tolroy manage?

MOSES: [*Gentle chuckle*] Poor Tolroy! Still, it don't take people long to settle to the basic necessities. Everybody got to eat, everybody got to sleep, everybody got to work, no matter what part of the world you come from... And talking about eating, it didn't take long for them shopkeepers and barrow boys to cash in on the immigration wave. Whatever district that the boys settle in, shops start to import all kinds of thing like dasheen and bread-fruit and hot pepper sauce. I tell you, whatever problems it have, many a shopkeeper must of bless the day immigration started, and bags of them must of made their fortunes dealing in these exotic fruits and vegetables and other stuff what you see our people queuing up for all over the place. It had a shop like that off the Harrow Road, where Tanty and Ma was living with Tolroy. It was pandemonium and chaos when you see all them West Indian housewives meet up in that shop, not only to buy goods, but to discuss topics of local interest, which is to say, discuss everybody's business but their own...

31

*In the shop, everyone wants service at the same time. The shopkeeper
can hardly cope. There are bursts of scandalized laughter, a hum of
conversation and loud demands for service...*

FIRST SHOPPER: Two pound of saltfish, please!

SECOND SHOPPER: You got any pigtails this week?

THIRD SHOPPER: These yams don't look too catholic... bests had cut
off that rotten end before you weigh it... What you was saying,
girl? She had the baby in the end?...

TANTY: [*Looking at some items on a shelf*] Ma! Look he have ackee!
But it inside a tin!

SHOPKEEPER: [*Distantly*] Ah, did you say ackee, madam? I imported
those especially for my customers. It's a new line.

TANTY: [*Loudly*] But why they put it in a tin? You ain't got fresh
ones?

SHOPKEEPER: The fresh ones don't keep, Tanty. They have to can
them. Helps to give your lot jobs in Jamaica, too. They're just as
good.

TANTY: How you know? You ever eat ackee?

MA: I going to buy a tin and try it out, anyway.

SHOPKEEPER: I also got fresh black-eye peas, cassava bread, brown
rice, and... look on the shelf you'll see tins of guava and soursop
juice... all for customers like you, Tanty, and Ma.

TANTY: [*In an undertone*] You hear what he say?

MA: Don't let him sweeten you up. We ain't got much money to
spend today.

SHOPKEEPER: What about some of these ripe plantains, Tanty?

TANTY: It would go good with the ackees and saltfish... What a
pound?

SHOPKEEPER: Four and six.

TANTY: Weigh a couple-few for me – about three.

MA: Don't buy too much things, Tanty.

TANTY: Ain't Tolroy getting pay today?

MA: We got the rent to pay, and money for the gas and electric.

TANTY: Don't worry, this shopkeeper is a nice man. You always
suspicious of everybody!

SHOPKEEPER: Anything else, madam?

TANTY: Yes. Two tins of guava, a pound of saltbeef, some red beans,
half a pound of saltfish – I don't want the tail part, eh, give me
from the top.

MA: [*In consternation*] You going mad today or what, Tanty?

TANTY: I tell you not to worry, We could take these things on trust. We been shopping here these past months, the gentleman must know us well by now.

MA: Trust! I don't think they give Credit in this country. Look at them two pictures the mister have up there on the wall.

TANTY: You mean Mr. Cash and Mr. Credit?

MA: That's right. You see how Mr. Credit limping with a crutch under his arm, and a bandage on his head?

TANTY: Yes. And look at Mr. Cash! He lolling back there in an arm chair with a big grin on his face and a cigar in his hand.

SHOPKEEPER: [*Returning to the counter*] There you are... Interested in those pictures are you? Genuine works of art, a real masterpiece of craftsmanship...

MA: [*Hastily*] We don't want to buy them, thank you!

TANTY: What you ought to do is take down those nasty pictures and put up something nice. Like the coronation of the Queen, or something.

SHOPKEEPER: [*Short laugh*] I like you, Tanty. You've got a sense of humour... What about some fresh salted mackerel? I've got a barrel at the back just opened.

TANTY: Bring it let me see.

MA: [*As the shopkeeper goes*] Tanty! You going to cause confusion here today, you know. Where you going to get the money to pay for all these things?

TANTY: I going to make him give us trust, that's what. And take down them two stupid pictures! Mr. Cash! Mr. Credit! That's not the way to treat regular customers.

SHOPKEEPER: [*Returning*] There... What do you think? One of these would weigh more then a pound!

TANTY: Give me four. And wrap them in plenty paper.

MA: Well I wash my hands of the whole thing. You going to land up in jail today self!

TANTY: You can't tell me, Ma! Ain't we have all that furniture on the H.P.?

MA: That's a different business.

TANTY: How different? People would trust you. You just wait till he come back...

SHOPKEEPER: [*Returning*] Will that be all? How about some...

MA: [*Quickly*] No, No! You better tot up all that and see what it come to!

TANTY: Yes... take one of those exercise books you have on the shelf there, and write down everything in it.

SHOPKEEPER: I'll just jot the list down on this piece of paper.

TANTY: [*Firmly*] No. Put it in the exercise book. And write my name and address on the cover.

SHOPKEEPER: Well... the book'll be sixpence extra?

TANTY: Never mind that.

SHOPKEEPER: All right... Let's see... red beans, two and six, black-eye, two and sixpence ha'penny.... There. Five pounds, eight shillings and eleven pence ha'penny. You want to check it?

There is a moaning sigh from Ma.

TANTY: No. I trust you. You don't trust me?

SHOPKEEPER: Sure I trust you Tanty!

TANTY: Good. You keep that exercise book safe, because every Friday, starting from next week please God, when Tolroy get pay, I will be coming into give you some money. Maybe not the full amount, but...

SHOPKEEPER: Here! Hold on! What's this?

TANTY: We call it trust back home. That way you keep all your customers happy.

SHOPKEEPER: You must be joking! Here, Ma, explain to Tanty that we don't do business like that in this country!

MA: Don't ask me! I not in this confusion at all!

SHOPKEEPER: If you're short of a few shillings, Tanty...

TANTY: All I got is half a crown. Look... [*She opens her purse to show and plonks coin on the counter*] You can have it as a deposit.

SHOPKEEPER: What do you think will happen to me if I 'trust' all my customers? I'll be like that chap in the picture there, limping.

TANTY: I don't know about the others, but you going to trust me, else I take my custom elsewhere. This is not the only shop on the Harrow Road, you know. And you wouldn't only lose me, I will take every West Indian customer with me.

SHOPKEEPER: Try and be reasonable, Tanty. It may be all right in Jamaica, but you won't get a shopkeeper here to do business that way...

Later, back at Tolroy's house. Ma and Tanty are cooking...

34

MA: [*Laughing*] ...You really good for yourself. I never thought he would of agreed.

TANTY: You got to teach them my child... Don't put in the ackee until the saltfish almost finish.

MA: It must be ready now [*Opens pot*] You want a taste to see how it going?

TANTY: Let me see… [*She tastes it*] ...Y-e-s, but I think it need a little more black pepper.

MA: All right... You not going to take the dirty clothes to the Bendix whilst I finish the lunch?

TANTY: Yes... [*She walks towards the door*] I don't know how Tolroy get those overalls so dirty... [*She tries the door*] You lock the door?

MA: No. The key not there on the ledge?

TANTY: No! You move it?

MA: [*Joining Tanty*] Oh lord! Don't tell me Tolroy gone to work with the key in his pocket!

TANTY: He must of left it on the breakfast table [*They both move back*] ... No, it not here.

MA: Look at my crosses!

TANTY: What we going to do?

MA: You have to go to the factory, Tanty. It not far.

TANTY: Me?

MA: You just catch a number 6 bus and ask them to drop you by the factory in Kensal Rise. All the conductors know it.

TANTY: You know I don't like these upstairs and downstairs buses.

MA: Well I got to get the children lunch ready when they come from school.

TANTY: [*Hesitant*] But how will I find Tolroy?

MA: Is not a big place! You sure to see him, or else Moses or Galahad. You could take some lunch for him and give him a surprise with the ackee...

In the factory, Moses and Galahad are packing away pot scourers in boxes.

GALAHAD: I tired packing away these blooming pot cleaners, Moses. I even dream them last night.

MOSES: Wait till you been here a few years like me.

GALAHAD: Is time I ask them for a raise, anyway.

35

MOSES: A raise! You only been here a few months, Galahad.

GALAHAD: I want to get some things for my room, man. This wage can't stretch far.

MOSES: You should praise the lord you get a work, and keep quiet.

GALAHAD: My room no old basement like yours. I got to keep it looking smart.

MOSES: You was grateful for the old basement when you first came though.

GALAHAD: Well, you know what I mean... [*He shifts one carton and pulls another*]... I intend to get on in Brit'n, boy.

MOSES: And I intend to get out... After pay today, guess what?

GALAHAD: What?

MOSES: Tropical gear, boy, tropical gear! White shoes! Cotton shirts! I got to get my kit ready for the tropics.

GALAHAD: [*Coolly disbelieving*] Oh that.

MOSES: Don't say 'oh that' as if you disbelieve me! You think is joke I making?

GALAHAD: You remind me of those wayside preachers back home who predict the world coming to an end every day.

MOSES: Is that what you think? You come with me this evening after work and see for yourself. I going straight to that shop in Portobello Road where Harris working. They have some sharp pieces of cloth there. Look... [*Takes out a list from his pocket*] I got a list of things I need. You could read?

GALAHAD: I don't want to see no list. But I will come this evening just for fun... This shop where Harris working, maybe they might have some vacancies?

MOSES: Shop work not easy to get. And you make more with overtime right here.

GALAHAD: I intend to prosper in Brit'n. I ain't going to spend the rest of my days making pot scourers.... It must have a lot of deals going on in this London town.

MOSES: How you mean deals?

GALAHAD: Deals, man, ways to make a few quick quid. A man like you who have been here so long should of had a Rolls, should of been living and dining at the Dorchester.

MOSES: You almost make me wish I could stay in Brit'n to see the day when a reprobate like you driving a Rolls and living high.

GALAHAD: You might still see the day. The rate you keep getting

36

out of the country, is a long time before you say farewell to Piccadilly.

MOSES: [*Disgustedly*] Ah-h, you!

Bob, an English friend of Moses, who lives in the same house, comes up.

BOB: Hey, Moses, you seen Tolroy around?

MOSES: He must be taking a break in the gents.

BOB: There's a smashing dame out by the gate to see him.

GALAHAD: Eh-heh? What she like?

BOB: One of the best, man. Out of this world.

GALAHAD: Blonde or brunette?

BOB: I was concentrating so much on her figure, I didn't notice... Whyn't you go and have a look?

GALAHAD: Anything to break this monotony... You could finish the lot off, Moses...

Galahad walks away. As he gets out of earshot, Bob bursts out laughing.

MOSES: What's the big joke, Bob?

BOB: Wait till Galahad sees the bird! She looks like Tolroy's grand-mother!

MOSES: [*Laughing*] Must be Tanty, or Ma... What'd she want?

BOB: I dunno... Where the hell is Tolroy?

MOSES: Give him a shout, Bob. He must of dozed off, like.

BOB: [*Pounding on the door of the gents*] Hey, Tolroy!

Sound off flushing toilet as the door opens.

TOLROY: I was just coming. You can't even have peace in the gents round here.

BOB: Somebody to see you at the gate. A real smasher. Where do you pick them up?

TOLROY: To see me? You sure?

BOB: Yeah... She's a bit early, isn't she? We don't get paid till after lunch.

TOLROY: [*Moving off*] To see me? I wonder who it is...

Tolroy goes out. As Bob and Moses are laughing, Galahad returns.

MOSES: What's she like, Galahad?

37

GALAHAD: Real sharp, man! Go and take a look. Tell him, Bob.

MOSES: Bob already told me.

GALAHAD: [*Crestfallen*] Oh…

MOSES: Let that be a lesson to you. Look, take that trolley back in the workshop. The foreman don't like them hanging around here.

GALAHAD: [*Going off with the trolley*] I will catch up with you for that one, Bob. You really had me that time. Smashing bird, huh!

BOB: You finish packing? I got to load the lorry.

MOSES: Just a few more boxes… Do us a favour this evening, Bob?

BOB: Sure.

MOSES: Pay my rent for me? You know how the damned landlord is when you're late, and I got to go out. I'll square you up when I come in.

BOB: Three pound ten, isn't it?

MOSES: Yes. Not posh like yours upstairs.

BOB: Where you off to? Another date?

MOSES: I got to get myself rigged out for my trip back home. You would dead in the heat wearing woollies and overcoat in Trinidad.

BOB: You all set this time?

MOSES: Praise the lord!

BOB: You better watch it. You must have a jinx or something, the way you keep putting it off all the time.

MOSES: I know is the biggest joke for the boys in Londontown, that's why I not making any big fuss this time. I shall fold my tent like the Arabs…

BOB: And your mosquito net!

MOSES: You know me so long and you still haven't been educated? The days for that are over.

BOB: Well I saw on the telly the other day about one of the islands, and they spoke about mosquitoes and malaria and typhoid.

MOSES: Sure they got that. But you ain't know it have diseases all over the world? Even in Great Brit'n? Ain't you got snakes here?

BOB: But no lions and tigers!

MOSES: Lord! You think it have lions and tigers in the West Indies? If I wasn't going back home soon, I would give you a course.

BOB: Take it easy. I was only taking the mickey.

MOSES: I hope so, because I find that people either think like you, or else they imagine sandy beaches, and nice blue water, and lazy lagoons, and the natives fussing around with rum punches and exotic fruits.

BOB: What's it really like in Jamaica, then?

MOSES: You see what I mean? Tell me something. You know London? You know Rome? In Italy? Well Trinidad, which is the island I come from, is about the same distance from Jamaica, a thousand miles away. You ever been in Rome?

BOB: No.

MOSES: Well I never been Jamaica. In fact, I never meet a Jamaican until I come to Brit'n.

BOB: Really?

MOSES: If I lie I die! It got plenty different islands, you see. We even talk different. When Tolroy come back I will ask him to give you some broad Jamaican... in fact [*Sound of footsteps approaching*] like he in a evil mood and talking some now!

TOLROY: [*Angrily and loudly as he approaches*] This raas-claat woman rarsing up a time...

MOSES: What happen, Tolroy?

TOLROY: This woman, man! Tanty! She gone and open up a account with the shop.

MOSES: [*Whistling in surprise*] She breaking new ground for the immigrants.

TOLROY: I tired telling she that she can't live in Brit'n like she live in Jamaica. But you think she will listen?

BOB: What's that she brought you, Tolroy?

TOLROY: [*Indicating parcel*] You mean this? Just some lunch.

BOB: Man, that's living! You even got lunch service laid on.

TOLROY: Don't believe I don't want my lunch hour though. You and Moses hurry back from the cafe and don't waste time drinking tea and smoking.

BOB: Let's have a look, Tolroy. Open it up.

TOLROY: What you want to see? Is only some steak and chips.

MOSES: [*Laughing*] Steak and chips! Bet you anything what he got there is some pigtail and peas and rice.

BOB: [*Playfully persistent*] Go on, Tolroy, open it up.

TOLROY: [*Backing off*] I told you it's steak and chips.

MOSES: Grab it, Bob!

BOB: You hold his hands!

There is a friendly tussle in which Bob gets the parcel.

TOLROY: Don't touch it, Bob!

BOB: Let's see this great steak and chips... [*He opens it*]

MOSES: You ever seen a steak and chips like that, Bob?

BOB: Give us a taste, Tolroy.

TOLROY: [*Snatching it back*] Go on! You English people won't even know good food when you see it!

MOSES: I won't advise you to taste, Bob. It must be full of hot pepper.

BOB: You mean chilli? I can eat hot.

MOSES: Don't rob old Tolroy. I tell you what. I will cook you a good peas and rice when I get home this evening, if you don't mind coming down and disgracing my basement.

BOB: That's a promise?

MOSES: Yes. You could see my tropical outfit at the same time... Aye, Tolroy, this man want to know if I taking a mosquito net with me! Tell the days for that finish.

TOLROY: What you going to do with a mosquito net in London?

MOSES: Not London, man. Take back with me to Trinidad.

TOLROY: Oh l-o-r-d... that theme still popular? Go on with Bob and have your fish and chips, man.

MOSES: [*To Bob*] You see what I tell you, Bob? I should of kept my blooming mouth quiet... Come on, look Galahad coming back. He and Tolroy could finish the packing.

GALAHAD: [*Coming up*] Ain't you going for lunch, Moses?

MOSES: [*Shortly*] Just going. Come on, Bob. These fellars always make a joke of everything. Just let them wait...

> As Moses and Bob walk out and reach some distance, Tolroy and Galahad shout after them.

TOLROY: Don't forget the mosquito net, Moses!

GALAHAD: You might need it to camp in Hyde Park in the summer! [*They burst out laughing*]

MOSES: [*From a distance*] Wait and see, that's all I say. Wait and see...

> Later that day, Moses and Galahad are standing outside the shop where Harris works, looking at the clothing displays.

GALAHAD: This the shop?

MOSES: Yes. Let's stand up here a while, I could see Harris tending to a customer. We'll wait till he finish.

Inside the shop, Harris is trying to sell a winter coat to a reluctant English customer.

HARRIS: ...you're lucky. These winter coats were held over, and actually, we're letting them go at a bargain price, actually.

CUSTOMER: That right?

HARRIS: Yes, Have a look at the lining... Observe the stitching. Notice the seams. Actually, in Saville Row, they had similar coats at fifty guineas during the winter months. Here in the Portobello Road we tend to be more human, actually.

CUSTOMER: [*Scowling*] Where'd you learn about winter clothes?

HARRIS: My dear man! I've been in this country for ages and ages. This is my home!

CUSTOMER: I'd still like to see the guv'nor.

HARRIS: [*Sighing*] Well, if you insist. Actually he's a bit busy at the moment.

CUSTOMER: Look mate, I don't intend to spend ten pounds unless I know what I'm buying... Even if you come from Saville Street.

HARRIS: Well, to be quite honest with you, old chap, I wasn't actually there, though with my credentials...

CUSTOMER: Ah, there's the guv'nor now... over there.

HARRIS: Yes... just a minute... [*He walks over to the proprietor*] Mr. Joseph, this customer is a bit insistent on seeing you himself...

MR. JOSEPH: Harris, I told you before that I or one of the other assistants would handle the white customers.

HARRIS: I can handle the sale, Mr. Joseph...

MR. JOSEPH: Look, there's a couple of your boys outside there. Do you know them?

HARRIS: Yes, it looks like my friend Moses and Galahad.

MR. JOSEPH: That's the one you said was coming in for some clothes? See that he buys something this time, Harris. He's always browsing around when he comes. Remember your wages depend on your sales.

HARRIS: Yes. About that customer...

MR. JOSEPH: Go on, man, get them inside!

Outside the shop.

MOSES: You see that shirt, Galahad? You notice the cut of the collar?

GALAHAD: That looks good to sport around in the evening after work... but I more interested in these household items... I didn't know they sell other things besides clothes...

HARRIS: [*Coming out*] Oh, certainly, Galahad. We cover a wide range to cater for everybody.

MOSES: Aye, Harris. How much is that bush jacket? The one in the corner?

GALAHAD: And that record player? I seriously interested. How many speeds it got?

HARRIS: You chaps are really serious? In making some purchases I mean.

MOSES: I don't know about Galahad, but as far as I am concerned, put it this way: I got one foot in Trinidad already! And I want you to rig me out with the best you got.

HARRIS: Very good. Very good! Come on in! What would you like to see first?

MOSES: [*They are in the shop now*] Your complete range.

HARRIS: Try on that bush jacket you saw in the window.

GALAHAD: About that record player...

HARRIS: See someone else, Galahad. I want to give Moses my undivided attention. Just step into this cubicle, old chap, and let me take your measurements...

Galahad wanders up to the stand with the record player. Joseph comes up to him.

MR. JOSEPH: A beauty isn't she? Three speeds too.

GALAHAD: It really nice. But forty pounds is a lot of money!

MR. JOSEPH: Don't bother about the price! Feel the smooth finish of the woodwork, Mr.... Mr. ...

GALAHAD: Galahad.

MR. JOSEPH: Mr. Galahad. Do you know, we've sold quite a few of these to your friends. In fact this particular one is from new stock. Would you like to try it out?

GALAHAD: Is no use. I haven't got forty pounds. I wish I had!

MR. JOSEPH: Oh, we can come to some arrangement about that. Let that be the least of your worries. Here. What would you like to hear? Some classical music? No, what am I saying! A calypso! We've got the very latest tunes from Jamaica.

GALAHAD: You got one from Trinidad?

MR. JOSEPH: Sure, sure! All our records are up to date. And you know what? You look like a serious customer. I'll let you have a record free with the player! What do you say?

GALAHAD: What I said already. I ain't got forty quid.

MR. JOSEPH: How much have you got? Can you put down five as a deposit?

GALAHAD: Well, I got five pounds.

MR. JOSEPH: You can pay off the rest in instalments... Of course, you'll have to have a guarantor...

GALAHAD: What's that?

MR. JOSEPH: Just someone to sign a form... a mere formality... Mr. Harris, perhaps? You know him?

GALAHAD: Not so well.

MR. JOSEPH: How about your friend?

GALAHAD: Moses?

MR. JOSEPH: Whatever his name is. It's nothing really. All your friends do it... I tell you what. You try the player out. Here. This is the starting switch. And this disc is the very latest calypso song they're singing in Jamaica... I mean Trinidad. Listen to the clarity and the tone, while I get you the forms...

Galahad puts the record on as Joseph goes to his office. Pick up calypso music...

MOSES: What's that, Harris? It sound like calypso.

HARRIS: Rather! I guess Galahad must be having a demonstration.

MOSES: Ah, that's all I need to put me in a good mood! With this bush jacket on, and this pair of flannels, and the sports shirt, I could shut my eyes and imagine I back home already.

HARRIS: You ought really to land in a light tropical suit, Moses. We've got something here I'd like to show you. I shan't be a tick...

MOSES: [*Musing*] Yes, Harris right. I don't want to land in Port of Spain no poor-me-one! First thing I think I'll do, is take a taxi straight off the ship, and cruise around town a little, looking up the old places, round by the Savannah, up Chancellor Hill, round by the Botanical Gardens. I mean, just imagine if one of my old friends see me in this taxi, smoking a cigar and watching the sights like a tourist! He will shout out, 'Aye, Moses! What you doing back in Trinidad, boy?' And me? I will only stop the taxi and say, 'Hop in George!' or 'Hop in, Chapman! I have left the cold, dismal climes of the Mother Country, and I am back home in my native land. No more hustling in Brit'n. I have come to rest my weary bones under a coconut tree, and listen to the waves on the beach!' And I could imagine Chapman might just stand up there, so surprise to see me, and he will say, 'So you made it at last, Moses!' And as if he can't believe his eyes, he will just keep on saying my name, 'Moses, Moses...'

GALAHAD: [*Interrupting this day dream*] Moses! I talking to you, man!

MOSES: Eh? What?

GALAHAD: This stupid man want me to have a witness.

MOSES: Don't interrupt me, Galahad. My mind is far away from here.

GALAHAD: Just sign this form for me, Moses. He say I got to have a witness.

MOSES: Witness? What for? Go away, man. You can't leave me in peace to savour my coming pleasures?

GALAHAD: For the record player... Just sign it like a friend, man, and do me a favour. Here, look, a pen. Just there... You yourself know how they have so many forms for everything in this country.

MOSES: I don't sign nothing unless I read it, boy.

GALAHAD: [*Exaggerated impatience*] The shop going to close any minute man! Look, it have a copy you could keep and read. Just sign it quick.

MOSES: A copy? Oh, all right, all right, there. Moses. You satisfy?

GALAHAD: Your full name, man! Moses Aloetta!

MOSES: [*Chuckling*] Everybody keep calling me Moses Moses, I even forget I had another name... There... What they want witness for?

GALAHAD: I don't know, man. They always have some stupidness in this country... Look the copy, you can keep that.

MOSES: Just push it in that new sports jacket pocket on the table there and leave me to my sightseeing... I will read it later. You know where I was? I just meet Chapman round the Savannah as I was cruising in a taxi, refreshing my memories... And right now, we going up by Laventille... I know Laventille good, boy, but look how it change... [*Galahad sneaks away as Moses sinks back into his reverie.*] ... Hear Chapman, 'Things not as you left them, Moses, it have big houses up on Laventille now...'

Galahad gives Joseph the form.

GALAHAD: Here you are, Mr. Joseph.

MR. JOSEPH: That wasn't much trouble was it? One thing I like about you people, is the way you look after each other.

GALAHAD: I could take it away now?

MR. JOSEPH: But of course! It's your property now. And don't forget your free record. Come again, anything you want, we have. Here, do you smoke? Have a cigar...

Later that day, Moses is knocking at the door of Bob's flat, eager to show off his new clothes.

BOB: [*Opening the door*] Hi, you back?

MOSES: Bob! Come on down and see my new clothes, boy!

BOB: All excited, eh? Guess I'd be too if I was going to the sun... How about the grub you promised me?

MOSES: I'll cook later... Come!

They go down the steps to Moses's basement flat and enter.

BOB: That lot must have set you back a few quid!

MOSES: Wait till you see the sports jacket, man! [*Rips the paper away*] I got to land up respectable, after all. I'm going back home... Just hold it for me and help me put it on, Bob... I haven't even got a bloody mirror in this room!

BOB: What's this in your pocket here? Your bill?

MOSES: Some old thing I sign for Galahad as witness... Throw it on the mantelpiece... And to go with the jacket, I got this pair of trousers... We don't have to match the trousers and the jacket back home, you know, and you could look real sharp... It's the jacket that...

BOB: Here, hold on! Did you read this?

MOSES: What?

BOB: This form you say you signed for Galahad. Do you know what it is?

MOSES: Why... What?

BOB: You've signed as guarantor for that man.

MOSES: Guarantor?

45

BOB: Yes! You know what that means? You're responsible for this record player.

MOSES: How could I be responsible?

BOB: If Galahad doesn't pay up, you will have to give them the money!

MOSES: [*Snatching the form from Bob*] Let me see that form! Oh Lord! Forty quid! That man must be mad! I going to tear up this damned thing.

BOB: Don't do that. You've already signed it. Didn't you read it?

MOSES: I wasn't even listening to what the man was saying! I was occupied there with my clothes... and he had the paper folded back just to where you sign... What this mean, Bob?

BOB: You ought to know Galahad by now. He's always up to some dodge in the factory.

MOSES: But... but... I ain't got no forty quid to spare!

BOB: He's put down five... but then, there'll be interest. It's as if you borrowed money. It's got to be paid back. You'd better see him and clear it up as soon as possible. Before you go, I mean.

MOSES: Before I go! Man, this thing going to make me postpone my trip! I can't take nothing out of my passage money at this stage!

BOB: It'll sort out... Look, let's go to the pub and have a drink. I got a couple of quid to spare, we can have some beer and grab some sausages in the pub. Forget about the cooking... Maybe you'll have another chance to cook me that peas and rice before you go...

PART THREE: MOSES RISKS AN INVESTMENT

REPORTER: So Moses, you had yet another set back to your plans for returning to Trinidad... It seems you were too trusting!

MOSES: I wouldn't say that exactly. Galahad manage to carfuffle me with that guarantor business, but that was the last time he took me in.

REPORTER: Then you got all set for the trip, afterwards?

MOSES: Not exactly... Don't forget I had other so-called friends... Cap, the wandering Nigerian, and Harris, and Big City, and Bart and the rest of them.

REPORTER: You mean somebody else took you for a ride this time?

MOSES: Not exactly... You see, it was summer, and when the old sun shinin' on Londontown, is as if the whole world change, and things don't look so grim as they did in the cold and the fog of winter. You could see them old geezers come to sit down in the park... and everywhere you turn you seeing the girls in summer frocks, and birds singing, and all the trees put back on their clothes, and even you yourself could sport a pair of cotton slacks and a hot shirt, and forget about the winter woollies and coats. The boys get on as if they gone mad, just dashing about town like blue flies: Big City give up his long-distance transport job and settle down in the Circus near to Eros, as if he mesmerise by the display of womanhood; Bart resume the search for a girl what he lost years ago; old Harris making contacts left and right for his annual summer dance and fete, and even Cap ambling around the West End to see what he could find. And at work, Galahad as if he can't stand still for one moment...

In the factory, sounds of machinery at work. Moses and Galahad are packing cartons of pot scourers. Galahad is humming and whistling a calypso...

MOSES: You in a good mood this morning, papa!

GALAHAD: You would of been too, if you put ten bob on a horse and you get back twenty quid... easy money, Moses. Easy as kissing hand.

MOSES: I prefer to do an honest day's work for my money, Galahad.

GALAHAD: Ah... I put you onto that second-hand car deal last week... You could of made an easy twenty-five.

MOSES: Any deal you in, you could count me out.

GALAHAD: Is no wonder you still hanging around the old Brit'n!

MOSES: You talking too much... Look, I finish packing three cartons to your one!

GALAHAD: On a day like today, how you expect a man to work? I should be outside in the wide open spaces, breathing fresh air and getting a tan and...

MOSES: Getting a tan, you say? You want to pass the point of invisibility?

GALAHAD: ...and I was going to say, with a nice English chick for company. This is the time of year when the lion got to roar!

MOSES: Good luck, good luck... I don't mind you talking if you like, but you think you could speed up a little with the packing? Instead of picking up one pot scourer at a time, try picking up two. Like me...

GALAHAD: Is time I had a bird, you know. I been keeping an eye on that thing in the cafe across the road.

MOSES: You mean Daisy?

GALAHAD: That's her name? I didn't even know. Daisy...

MOSES: Well I don't see why a smart man like you who always up to something can't find a woman.

GALAHAD: I am shy with women.

MOSES: [*Laughing*] You! Shy! A bold, brass-face reprobate like you shy?

GALAHAD: I been giving her a little sweet-eye now and then, but I don't think she notice... You know her?

MOSES: Everybody in the factory know Daisy, man!

GALAHAD: You can't put in a good word for me?

MOSES: I wouldn't even put in a bad one! If you so rusty, find you own woman! And hurry up, look Bob going for tea and we ain't finish this lot yet!

BOB: [*Walking up to them*] Coming for a cup of tea, Moses?

MOSES: I want to finish this, Bob.

BOB: You been at that since morning!

MOSES: Well with old Speedy here, you know what it like.

GALAHAD: If you not going, I'll go.

MOSES: You might as well, I wouldn't miss you. I'll join you and Bob when Tolroy comes.

BOB: As long as you buy your own tea, Galahad.

GALAHAD: [*As he and Bob walk away*] I'll even treat you to a cuppa, Bob, and a bun. Listen, you know that girl in the cafe? Daisy...?

A little later. Bob and Galahad are sitting in the cafe...

BOB: That wasn't a bad bun.

GALAHAD: Have another! What about them sausage rolls? You'd like another?

BOB: I already had two!

GALAHAD: Well, another tea... you know her well?

BOB: Who? Daisy? Sure.

GALAHAD: She not so bad, you know... I been keeping an eye on her.

BOB: You interested?

GALAHAD: I wouldn't mind getting an introduction...

BOB: [*Laughing*] Hell, she knows everybody in the factory! Ain't you ever spoken to her all this time you've been coming?

GALAHAD: Only for a cup of tea or so... I a bit shy with the girls, Bob,

BOB: You shy! Oh come on, Galahad!

GALAHAD: No, seriously... I want you to try and make a date for me, Bob, to take her to the pictures or something.

BOB: Your big mouth usually works.

GALAHAD: Not with women. Call she. Have another cup and a sandwich.

BOB: I don't trust you, Galahad. I don't want to be involved, innocent as it seems.

GALAHAD: I am rusty, man! I haven't taken out a girl since I came to London.

BOB: Too busy making a fast quid or two, eh?

GALAHAD: I tell you what I'll do, Bob. You scratch my back, I scratch yours. Right?

BOB: What d'you mean?

GALAHAD: Well, you always talking about how you like coloured girls, not so?

BOB: So what?

GALAHAD: So you fix me up with Daisy, and I fix you up with a lovely thing from St. Lucia. She… am… not in the country long. She would love a white boyfriend. Honest.

BOB: You just said you can't get on with the birds?

GALAHAD: That's the English ones, man. I mean, chicks from back home, I got them by the dozen. I could get you two if you want.

BOB: Hmm… What's her name?

GALAHAD: Everybody call her Tant… I mean Lucy. Yes.

BOB: You don't even know her name for sure.

GALAHAD: I just told you. A real smasher, Bob. She live off the Harrow Road… Yes, she would be just the one for you. What you say?

BOB: Suppose Daisy isn't interested in going out with you?

GALAHAD: Let's try, man… I'll call her and order some more tea, and you talk… [*Raising his voice*] Miss! A minute please!

DAISY: [*Coming over*] Not more tea! Bob, you had six cups between you two already!

GALAHAD: Yes please, two more *cups*… [*In an undertone to Bob*] Go on, man! Introduce me or something.

BOB: My friend Galahad here is the thirsty one… You don't know him?

DAISY: [*Indifferently*] I seen him around.

BOB: Says he likes you… Don't know why, meself! Wants to take you out for an evening on the town… You name it, Galahad can supply it. The Savoy, a theatre show… dancing to soft lights in one of the more expensive spots… Ain't that so, Galahad?

GALAHAD: [*Tongue-tied*] Uh-huh.

DAISY: Talks a lot, doesn't he?

GALAHAD: [*Bucking up nerve, clearing his throat*] Action speak louder than words.

DAISY: [*Coyly*] I like a man who does things… You really been to the Savoy? What as, a dishwasher? [*She laughs*]

GALAHAD: When I get in there, somebody else would be washing my dishes!

DAISY: Where's Moses this morning, Bob?

BOB: He should be here in a minute… I got to go, Galahad, coming?

GALAHAD: In a little while… [*Bob goes; Galahad is feeling a little bolder*] You ever been in the Savoy?

DAISY: That'll be the day. Them sorts of places aren't for the likes of me... You like it, in the factory?

GALAHAD: I got more ambition than that! I got some big deals in the fire.

DAISY: Such as?

GALAHAD: Well... How about Sunday evening? You doing anything?

DAISY: Depends.

GALAHAD: We could have a nice time. I not mean like some fellars.

DAISY: I'm not promising nothing, mind you. We'll see... Cafe opens Sunday too, but I could get some time off.

Sunday evening, Hyde Park Corner: the sounds of crowds and indistinct public speakers.

MOSES: Ah Cap-oh! How you go, bo?

CAP: Moses! So-so, bo!

MOSES: What happening, man? I ain't seen you since you shift from the Water, owing that landlady eight pounds.

CAP: How you hear about that?

MOSES: I pass round one evening to see you, and she tell me. In fact, she swear she would never take another coloured tenant. You muddying the water for the boys.

CAP: I will pay her one of these days, please God. I am waiting on my allowance from Nigeria.

MOSES: What happen? Your tribe paying you to keep away?

CAP: [*Chuckling*] *My* uncle has sold some land and made a big profit

MOSES: Well, don't forget your friends in your prosperity, Cap. Remember all them pig-foot and dumpling you knock back in my basement. And that old winter coat that I gave you when you was bawling for your mother in that London particular... I learn that phrase from Harris.

CAP: How Harris? I thought I seen him boarding a bus down by Latimer Road the other day. But it couldn't of been him in that dismal part of town.

MOSES: It might have been

CAP: Boy, I miss the Water too bad,

MOSES: Where you staying now, then? I mean, at the moment, like?

CAP: Earl's Court. I found a wealthy Russian widow.

MOSES: Man lucky! How something like that could never happen to me? She paying the rent?

CAP: But of course! Only till I get my allowance, though. In the meantime... [*Fishes in his pocket*] have a look at this old watch. You interested?

MOSES: I got a wristwatch already.

CAP: Pity. It going cheap, even though it's a Russian heirloom. You can't get a watch like that these days... You don't want to lend me a half-crown and hold it as security? [*Moses is silent*] Well... [*Fishes out a ring*] Look at this ring. Just look at it.

MOSES: What's this writing on it?

CAP: Russian. I not selling that ring, though, not for a hundred pounds... [*Pause*] Try it on if you like... It fit you?

MOSES: It a bit tight... Here, look your ring, Cap. I cannot depart with even a half a crown these days. Look around for one of the other boys.

CAP: Oh well... Never mind... Aye, look that coloured American fellar going to talk over there! Let's listen to some politics...

SPEAKER: ...and the trouble in this country, my friends, has nothing to do with the industrial situation. If you did not bring in immigrants, your buses would be in the garage, your trains would never leave the stations, your hospitals would have to shut down because there would be nobody to run them. I tell you, my friends that unless you learn to live in peace and harmony this country will go, to the dogs...

CAP: You not interested in politics, Moses?

MOSES: Ah, what's the use of *talking?* Come on, man, let's take a walk...

CAP: Still boy, I interested in politics, you see. We got to start doing something in Brit'n, you know, else we get left behind.

MOSES: Cool it, man, cool it... Look at that thing over there. You slacking, Cap! She on her own, too.

CAP: Um-um! Look like a continental... She got an A-Z in her hand. You coming?

MOSES: You carry on... As if I see old Galahad coming across the park there...

Cap goes off after the girl. Galahad comes up with Daisy. He is full of beans.

GALAHAD: Moses! Look at the sun, man! Watch how green the grass is! Summer is hearts in Londontown, boy! If you see them couples laying down on the ground, and under the trees!

MOSES: [*Ignoring him*] Hi Daisy! You trusting yourself with this man?

DAISY: Hello, Moses!

MOSES: How's he treating you?

DAISY: He's made a lot of promises, but we haven't done a thing so far but walk around.

GALAHAD: Relax, Daisy! We got the whole evening ahead of us. Relax and enjoy our city on a balmy summer's evening.

MOSES: What happened to your Jag, Galahad?

GALAHAD: It's in the garage at the moment, some trouble with the back axle... Any interesting speakers around?

MOSES: None that could shoot a line better than you, old man.

GALAHAD: Don't listen to him, Daisy. He just talk, but he got a heart of gold. Here, have a cigar.

MOSES: Oh, cigar, is it? Don't mind if do... Some of us got to roll our own...

GALAHAD: [*As they light up*] Who is that coming there? Cap?

MOSES: Yes, he went to tackle a thing... [*As Cap comes up*] Any luck Cap?

CAP: No, bo. I lost her in the crowd... What happening Galahad? Like things going good with you!

GALAHAD: Have a good Havana, Cap. Surprise your lungs.

CAP: Thanks, bo...

GALAHAD: And meet Daisy... You don't know the old Cap?

DAISY: No... Hello.

GALAHAD: He is a chieftain from Nigeria. His father rules ten tribes.

CAP: Not ten. Eleven.

GALAHAD: Oh yes, I keep forgetting.

DAISY: [*Seriously*] Is that true?

CAP: Well, not really a chieftain yet. I am waiting for my father to die... But that might happen any day now.

DAISY: I don't believe you! Is it true, Moses?

MOSES: All I can tell you about Cap, Daisy, is that he manage to get by no matter how hard things are.

CAP: That's a nice ring you got on. Where you get it?

DAISY: Oh, it's nothing. I picked it up in Woolworths.

CAP: As you mention rings, I happen to have a couple of trinkets on me... Try this Russian heirloom on. [*Shows her the ring*]

DAISY: [*With bated breath*] Russian heirloom! Where'd you get it?

CAP: I spent a few days in Moscow last week... Does it fit?

DAISY: [*Excited*] Yes! Look at this, Galahad! Isn't it pretty?

GALAHAD: You like it?

DAISY: It's smashing!

GALAHAD: How much, Cap?

CAP: I never said anything about selling, Galahad.

GALAHAD: How much? A quid?

CAP: A quid! Good lord! Listen to this man, Moses! A quid for my Russian heirloom!

MOSES: It's worth at least two... guineas. Go on, Galahad. Don't tell me you can't afford a little thing like that? For Daisy?

GALAHAD: Two quid won't bust me... Here, Cap, live and let live, eh?

CAP: It's only as it's you I letting it go so cheap, Galahad. Otherwise it would of been a fiver at least.

DAISY: Oh! You really shouldn't, Galahad! Thanks... Is it real diamonds?

CAP: Hold it up to the sun and you will see the colours... Galahad, I got a gold watch here...

GALAHAD: Don't press your luck, old man. You catch me in a good mood this evening... Look at that big crowd over there. I wonder what that fellar talking about?

DAISY: We're not just going to stand around here all evening, are we, Galahad?

GALAHAD: I just want to listen a little bit... I always surprise how these fellars say all kinds of things against the Queen and country and get away with it, Coming, Moses?

MOSES: Well, only for the walk.

He and Galahad go.

DAISY: [*Impatient*] Oh! If I thought this was how I was going to spend the evening, I'd never have come!

CAP: You like the ring?

DAISY: Yes, it fits as if it was made for me...

CAP: I pick up these odd things on my travels... What part of London you live?

DAISY: Kensal Rise... I wish Galahad would hurry! I want to go to the West End.

CAP: Once the boys start listening to politics, you can't drag them away...

DAISY: I've half mind to go off and leave him, honestly!

CAP: It have a coffee shop across the road there, by the Arch. Let's have a cup instead of just standing here.

DAISY: Well... I could do with something to eat. And drink. And my feet are killing me.

CAP: Come on then. He and Moses will be there all evening... What part of the West End did you have in mind?

DAISY: We were going to the pictures or something...

CAP: [*They start walking*] There's a good film on at the Odeon in Leicester Square.

DAISY: What're you doing in London, then?

CAP: I'm taking a course in government administration. When I go back home I will have to rule more than a million people...

They exit. Enter Moses and Galahad. Bob walks up to join them.

BOB: Ah! I thought I'd meet you blokes here on a Sunday evening!

MOSES: What you know, Bob? Taking a stroll?

BOB: I was looking for this Galahad in particular! You call that funny, I suppose?

GALAHAD: [*All innocent*] What, Bob?

BOB: Sending me to the Harrow Road on a blind date with Tolroy's Tanty!

MOSES: What! [*Bursts out laughing*] You mean that was the date you told me he fixed for you? Galahad tell you something and you believe him?

GALAHAD: [*Laughing too*] You got to admit it got a funny side!

BOB: Yeah... funny for you... I wasted a whole evening.

GALAHAD: Here, have a cigar, Bob, no hard feelings.

MOSES: [*Still chuckling*] I can't help laughing... What did Tanty say?

BOB: Luckily Tolroy came to the door, and as soon as I saw him I suspected this bastard was having me on. Tolroy confirmed my suspicions.

GALAHAD: Let me light your cigar for you, Bob... Look, I'll give you a telephone number, Bayswater...

BOB: No thank you. I'll get my own birds, my own way... Where's Daisy, then?

55

GALAHAD: Somewhere behind there waiting... We was just listening to this fellar blasting away at the Mother Country. One thing over here, boy, we got freedom of speech.

MOSES: Yes, but not to be confused with them tall tales you always spinning.

BOB: Yeah... you're good, boy, good. You ought to be up on a box yourself.

GALAHAD: You think so?

BOB: Sure, you could tell them a thing or two.

GALAHAD: I not bad at making speeches, you know.

MOSES: That's a good idea, Galahad. You go up there and instruct them. You know how ignorant the people in Brit'n are, you could teach them a thing or two.

GALAHAD: Well... I haven't got a platform, have I?

BOB: There you are, Moses! When it comes down to brass tacks, he chickens out!

MOSES: What you want with platform? Look they asking for guest speakers over there from the crowd...

GALAHAD: And Daisy... she must be getting impatient.

BOB: Why don't you be honest and say you're scared stiff?

MOSES: Never mind Daisy, I will bring her to hear you give a brilliant oration... Come on...

Moses drags Galahad through the crowd to the front...

MOSES: Excuse me please... ta... My friend here is going to address you... yes... excuse, please... Mind your backs... Make way for Sir Galahad!

To encouraging shouts from the crowd, Galahad stumbles up the small platform ladder and stands. He has lost all his cockiness. He is frequently drowned by shouts from the crowd.

GALAHAD: [*In a small squeaky voice at first, which he clears...*] I.... I.... I...

CROWD VOICE: Aye-aye!

GALAHAD: Ladies and gentlemen, my friends...

BOB: What friends?

GALAHAD: First and foremost, what I would like to say about the situation, is that it is not entirely one of despair. It is not without hope. Give and take has always been my motto, you scratch my back, I scratch yours...

MOSES: [*Aside*] Hear the old vagabond! He don't know what he talking about!

BOB: [*Laughing*] I'm enjoying this! Wish they'd drag him off, and ... how do you say it?

MOSES: Beat him like a snake! Wash him with licks!

BOB: I got a sneaking liking for him, though. He's got the guts to stand up there, not having the slightest clue.

MOSES: Ah, he only went there because we push him... [*Shouting to Galahad*] Tell them about *our* difficulties, man! The housing situation! The trouble to get jobs!...

GALAHAD: If I did not have so much interruption from the crowd, I could make my point.

CROWD VOICE ONE: Yeah, and sit on it!

CROWD VOICE TWO: Take him away!

There are boos and jeers from the crowd: Galahad descends and makes his way to Moses and Bob.

GALAHAD: They wouldn't give me a chance, as you seen for yourself. Otherwise...

MOSES: [*Jeering*] Yeah, otherwise you would of set the whole country right, wouldn't you?

BOB: Moses is only jealous, Galahad. I thought you were great.

GALAHAD: In truth? If I did really get under way...

BOB: The only thing is I didn't get what you were talking about.

GALAHAD: They didn't give me a chance... As a matter of fact I thought I recognise your voice... and Moses among the hecklers.

MOSES: We were only trying to encourage you, man!

GALAHAD: What Daisy think?... Where she gone?

MOSES: Let we look for her... She somewhere around...

A little later, after a fruitless search...

GALAHAD: But this is a hell of a thing, man! I can't see this woman anywhere! You say you left she with Cap? I can't trust that man, you know!

MOSES: I agree. You don't know who is your friend and who is your enemy in Londontown, countryman or no countryman... They must of taken off for the West End...

57

GALAHAD: Yes, that's it! If we walk up Oxford Street we should catch up with them.

BOB: I'm not going that way, Moses. I got to see my contact about that job in Earl's Court...

GALAHAD: You leaving the factory?

MOSES: Bob don't have to stick in no job. He could always get something to do.

GALAHAD: What new job is this, Bob?

BOB: Some exhibition they're putting on... always something going, with these shows.

GALAHAD: You think they have room for me?

BOB: They want workers, mate... What time you're coming home, Moses?

MOSES: I'll just take a cruise up the West End with Galahad, seeing that he holding big with all the money he flashing. I got to get back as much as I could from this man, even if it's just a coffee or a bus fare!

BOB: Give us a look-up if you get in before midnight...

MOSES: Right. See you, Bob...

Bob leaves, and Moses and Galahad saunter along Oxford Street...

GALAHAD: Whenever these fellars see a white girl with a man, they feel they could get in, too... Why the hell Cap went off with my girl?

MOSES: Relax, man. You ask Daisy that when you see her... Enjoy the balmy summer evening... You have any more of them Havanas?

GALAHAD: Only a few that I saving.

MOSES: Let's smoke, man. Look big, like an American. You never know your luck, you might pick up a thing as we strolling... One just as good as another.

GALAHAD: All right. Here. [*He gives him a cigar and they pause to light up*] I shouldn't of bought she that ring off Cap... I about three pounds down and I ain't get anything yet, not even a kiss... Where do you think she gone with Cap? You think he take she to his place?

MOSES: Who knows? Cap is a fast worker... He don't waste time. I tell you what. You look on the other side of the street as we

58

walking, and I look here. And if you see any infant window-shopping, don't be afraid to tackle her! A bird in the hand is worth ten in the bush, man! You could always date Daisy another time...

They stroll on...

GALAHAD: Moses! I seen somebody in that teashop you just passed. You not searching properly, man.

MOSES: Who?

GALAHAD: One of us. Reading the *Sunday Times.* It look like Harris.

MOSES: Most probably... Let's go back and ask he if he seen them...

They enter the tea shop and join Harris...

HARRIS: Hello Moses! What a pleasure to see you! And Galahad! Draw up a pew, old chap!

MOSES: Yeah... Order some coffee from the waitress, Galahad.

GALAHAD: It cheaper if I go to the counter myself... You got yours, Harris?

HARRIS: [*Quickly*] It's a bit cold now, Galahad. I wouldn't object to another.

MOSES: [As *Galahad goes off*] You seen anything of Cap?

HARRIS: Why yes! He was here a short while ago, with a friend... As a matter of fact, I took advantage of a bargain watch he happened to have on him... here... [*Takes the watch out*] What do you think of it?

MOSES: What did you pay for it?

HARRIS: I thought it cheap at the price. Ten shillings?... Hello! It's stopped working! It was going fine when he gave me...

GALAHAD: [*Coming back with the coffee*] Harris seen them, Moses?

MOSES: Yeah... They was here a little while ago.

GALAHAD: You know where they gone, Harris?

HARRIS: I really couldn't say, old boy. Though I heard his companion urging him along to the pictures.

GALAHAD: What pictures? What theatre?

HARRIS: Oh come now, Galahad! You didn't expect me to listen to their private conversations?

GALAHAD: [*Clanging cup on saucer angrily*] I'm going after them! You coming, Moses?

MOSES: Let me finish my coffee, man. In any case, you might as well give up this quest and relax. You can't find them now.

GALAHAD: I going to try. I don't want Cap to think he pull a fast one on me... Harris, how long they left?

HARRIS: [*Consulting his watch*] Let's see... Oh bother, I forgot that it's stopped... Couldn't have been very long, though. I'd say six or seven minutes...

GALAHAD: Well I off. [*Draws back his chair angrily and gets up*] The first time a man had a date with a white bird... Just let me catch up with that blooming Nigerian... [*He goes*]

HARRIS: Well Moses! I don't know how you tolerate these chaps... But I suppose you got that cigar off him?

MOSES: I intend to get back as much as I could from Galahad, by foul means or fair.

HARRIS: But I don't suppose you're allowing these little trivialities to obstruct your main objective of returning to the Caribbean?

MOSES: Oh, that's fixed. Any day now...

HARRIS: Exactly. I wish I were in your shoes... [*Sighs*] What wouldn't I do for a few months in my native land! The Britons don't appreciate how genuine visitors like you and me long to return to the friendliness and warmth of the islands... We are all, alas, considered as a mass of immigrants, and individuals like you and me become lost in the general conception... You have a certain amount of *Reserve*, of course?

MOSES: Reserve?

HARRIS: I mean, you're not going to return home as a pauper? You've got a bit of extra capital for emergencies and unforeseen circumstances?

MOSES: Man, home is home. I got friends. I got aunts and uncles that I could stay by until I get on my feet.

HARRIS: You have to be careful, boy. Have you had news from home recently?

MOSES: Not really. I want to land up sudden and surprise them, like.

HARRIS: I know exactly how you feel. But we have got to face the facts, you know. I myself am in constant contact with the situation at home, and I can tell you, Moses, that it would be a terrible mistake to arrive there and hope for the best.

MOSES: [*Getting uneasy*] How you mean?

HARRIS: Reserve, old top, Reserve! Let us take a hypothetical case...

MOSES: Don't use no big words with me.

HARRIS: Well, let us assume you return home and find things difficult.

MOSES: You mean like I can't find a place to live?

HARRIS: Exactly.

MOSES: And I can't get a work?

HARRIS: Exactly.

MOSES: And I hustling in Trinidad the same way I hustled in the old Brit'n?

HARRIS: You're getting the idea.

MOSES: That would be calamity! Disaster! Catastrophe! [*Uneasy laugh*] Harris, you was the last man I thought would try to put me off...

HARRIS: I only have your own welfare at heart, dear chap. If you haven't budgeted for a reserve, for your own security, you will be quite lost if such eventualities arise...

MOSES: I see... What you really mean is that apart from my passage and a few extra pounds, what I already have, I ought to think of the future?

HARRIS: Now you're cooking with gas, as our American friends say... Have you such a Reserve put by?

MOSES: To tell the truth, no.

HARRIS: Then in an emergency, you will find yourself wishing you had never left the shores of the Mother Country, believe you me.

MOSES: [*Pauses briefly*] Boy, you really set me thinking. I was just concerned about getting out of Brit'n; I didn't think about all that.

HARRIS: Exactly. Now, I will do you a favour, Moses. I will give you the benefit of my experience and learning. But not only that, I will offer you a helping hand in your troubles.

MOSES: I had enough of that. I don't intend to listen to anything you have to say. I holding onto the money I have like a miser.

HARRIS: My dear chap, that's your trouble. With intelligent investment you can double or treble your capital!

MOSES: You mean like stocks and bonds?

HARRIS: Well, that's an example, though since the stock market at the moment fluctuates at an alarming rate, you would be ill-advised to venture your money in that direction. Nor would I ask you to squander your hard-earned savings on such capricious ventures as horse-racing or the football pools, like those other layabouts.

MOSES: What then?

HARRIS: You want something solid, something that cannot fail, that has proved itself year after year. In other words, you want to be one hundred percent sure that your investment is in the right hands.

MOSES: They have such a thing as that?

HARRIS: That's the bother... I'm racking my brains, but the only solution I can come up with, is a rather personal one.

MOSES: Ah! I see!

HARRIS: Of course, it would mean that I shall have to turn down one of my backers, but for you, Moses, I will take the risk of seriously offending him... Yes, it will be worth it, to see you securely on your way.

MOSES: You getting me suspicious. You talking like Galahad with one of his deals.

HARRIS: You shock me Moses! What I have in mind is no fly-by-night affair. Actually, I'm not sure if I can manipulate it.

MOSES: Well, make your point, man! What is the big deal?

HARRIS: What else but 'HARRIS'S ANNUAL DANCE AND FETE'? What could be a more secure investment than that in the whole of Great Britain? Let me remind you, Moses, that the chaps come from as far afield as Birmingham and Manchester to attend one of my dos. Year after year it has been a grand success, so much so that I am flooded with backers who want to invest a small amount... say fifty pounds or so?

MOSES: I got to admit you do have a lot of people attending...

HARRIS: But of course! This summer, I have decided on St. Pancras Town Hall because it is one of the largest in the city, and can accommodate the large numbers who will be flocking to King's Cross from Brixton to the Black Country. My dear fellow, you have no idea!

MOSES: H'mm... if you think for a moment that you tempting me, you better think again. I have fallen prey to too many schemes in Londontown, and been left with the sticky end time and again. Not Moses Aloetta, boy!

HARRIS: Scheme! Good gracious, old fellow, you're not comparing my activities with the nefarious doings of rogues like Sir Galahad and the Captain? ... I... I... feel insulted. I really do!

MOSES: Nothing personal. Is just that once bitten, twice shy.

HARRIS: You'll never find a concrete investment like this. What can you lose? And think of what you'll gain! Let's see... I cleared four hundred pounds last year, after expenses, and that was in a small place in Ladbroke Grove, you'll remember...

MOSES: [*Whistling astonishment*] As much as that!

HARRIS: Of course it was split up among the investors. Naturally those who put in more money, get more return.

MOSES: Well suppose, just suppose, eh, nothing more... suppose I invest fifty pounds?

HARRIS: Offhand I'd say that would be doubled.

MOSES: You mean a hundred for my fifty?

HARRIS: Give or take a few pounds, yes.

MOSES: Well, well! And if I put about seventy-five in the fete?

HARRIS: Your profits go up, naturally. Let me explain it to you as simply as I could, old boy. Let's assume we get a crowd of five hundred odd. Now you multiply that by...

Later that night. Moses is knocking on Bob's door.

MOSES: [*All excited*] Bob! You there!

BOB: Moses? Come in...

MOSES: [*Entering*] Great news, boy. I really think I am on to something at last.

BOB: Oh? That'll make a change for you, mate!

MOSES: This is serious. I have invested in that dance Harris giving at St. Pancras next month.

BOB: Oh no, Moses! What'd you put yourself in for?

MOSES: I can't lose, Bob. Harris explain everything to me. I invest fifty, I get back a hundred.

BOB: You mean you're digging into the money you've been saving with blood and sweat for your trip?

MOSES: I got to have a Reserve, you see. In case of emergency. Let me explain it to you. Suppose something go wrong when I get back to Trinidad....

PART FOUR: HARRIS SPRINGS A FETE

REPORTER: . . .So, Moses, how did Harris's dance work out? I imagine you made a big profit.

MOSES: Depends on what sort of profit you mean. I profit, in the sense that I emerge from the whole affair a wiser man.

REPORTER: And what did Harris give you for your fifty pounds? Enough to take care of any eventualities that might have turned up when you returned to Trinidad? That was your worry, wasn't it?

MOSES: It's a worry that still exist!

REPORTER: You mean things didn't work out for you? What happened?

MOSES: The way how things started up that summer night in St. Pancras, I really thought that at last Fortune was going to smile on me after all my travails and hardships in the old country. I stand up there in front of the Town Hall with Harris that night, counting the customers as they go in. You could imagine Harris, in tuxedo suit, with his hair well greased back, and a beaming smile on his face as the crowd growing thicker and thicker. I had on that light suit I did buy to land home in – I thought I might as well give it a try out in Brit'n – and I was counting too, because fifty quid of my blood and sweat money, as Bob call it, was invested. And old Harris greeting all the English people with a pleasant good evening and how do you do, and a not so pleasant greeting for the boys, for the thing that was bothering him most was that the boys might get high and turn the dance into a brawl. As far as I was concern, I didn't care who and who came, as long as they buying and swelling my profit. Well, everybody turn up that night. Big City arrive with five white chicks holding onto him, Bart at last recover the girl he did lost and put in an appearance, Cap come rigged up in the national costume of a

64

Nigerian chieftain, and when I look for Tolroy, guess what? Tolroy had Tanty on one arm and Ma on the other, and the bird he bring had was to walk in front! Behind me and Harris I could hear things starting to warm up quickly: the steel band was playing even before people arrive. Galahad was the last man in, and I hardly recognise him, he was dress so flashy, with a big cigar in his mouth and a white chick on each arm. Since he left the job in the factory, he must of done some big deals. You know the saying that the devil look after his own? Well, the devil was looking after Galahad... I was only waiting then for Bob, and I let him pass in free. I mean, people could say what they like, but Bob was always good to me, and I did rather pass him in free than any of those scoundrels and vagabonds who call themselves my friends. By the time the rush start to thin out, and only stragglers was coming in, I was anxious to go in the office and count the takings, but old Harris still stand up there rubbing his hands together and smiling, as if he wish he could use mental telepathy and bring the whole population of Londontown into St. Pancras Town Hall...

In front of the Town Hall Steps, muted steel band music in the background...

MOSES: [*Impatiently*] Come on, man Harris. Let's count the money.

HARRIS: Don't be so avaricious old bean. There are still a few special invitees I am waiting for.

MOSES: Well, I going inside, man. Give me a call when you are ready.

HARRIS: Yes, you do that... and Moses, keep an eye on those chaps for me, will you? Especially Big City. I've a feeling he will be smoking those disgusting cigarettes.

MOSES: If you want to employ me as a floor walker you got to pay me.

HARRIS: Just see that they behave themselves, there's a good chap...

Inside the hall there is uproar; the steel band is blasting out; there are shouts and scandalous laughter. Moses heads for the bar where he meets Bob...

MOSES: Ah, Bob! I thought I would meet you at the bar. What a pandemonium here tonight, eh!

BOB: Well, it's in your favour, mate. You can't stick a pin in that crowd. Looks like you made a good investment after all.

MOSES: Well one thing I know for sure is that Harris wouldn't try to pull a fast one on me... What you drinking?

BOB: Draught bitter.

MOSES: I going to have a large rum... Get my throat accustom to home drink again... [*To bartender*] A pint of draught bitter, please, and a large rum – Barbados rum if you have it...

BOB: Cheers, Moses. Almost like a farewell party for you, eh?

MOSES: In a way, I suppose so... but I will be going to many such fetes in Trinidad. That is the land of fete, boy...

BOB: You on night shift now? I haven't been seeing you.

MOSES: Day and night. What about you, still at Earl's Court?

BOB: That was only a temporary job putting up the exhibition. I'm at the Town Hall now. A messenger.

MOSES: Boy, I wish I could of moved around like you do!

BOB: Oh, I don't know. We're about the same age. I feel like settling down same as you feel like getting back home... Maybe I will if this messenger job's any good.

MOSES: Get married and raise a few picc'ns, eh? That's the best thing, boy. No use carrying on like this day after day... It ain't got no future... [*Finishes his drink*] Lord! That rum surprise my belly!

BOB: Have another surprise... [*To bartender*] Same again, please... You're not dancing? Didn't you bring anybody?

MOSES: I'll make out all right on my own... I just want to steam up with a few drinks first. Then I will scout around the hall...

In the middle of the dance floor, Galahad is persuading Daisy to dance to a calypso...

DAISY: Of course I like it, Galahad, it makes me want to dance!

GALAHAD: Well come on, Daisy. I tell you it not hard. I will teach you the steps.

DAISY: I don't think I could wiggle my bottom like that... I've got a tight corset on...

GALAHAD: Well go to the ladies and slacken it. Don't stay long, I waiting just in this corner...

As Daisy goes, Cap comes up...

CAP: How you go, bo?

GALAHAD: Aye, Cap, you look impressive in that African gear. Boy! What is that?

CAP: Well, this headpiece is the main thing... it denote my rank. And this purple stripe on the gown, that say what tribes I rule.

GALAHAD: Is that right? You must be fooling a lot of English people, eh?

CAP: This is a genuine costume, no fears!

GALAHAD: You must get one like that for me... It might come in useful one time, you never know.

CAP: If you interested, I could let you have this one second hand.

GALAHAD: We'll talk business later... What the hell happen to Daisy? They got a queue at the ladies?

CAP: Is that where she is? I thought I could have a set with her.

GALAHAD: [*Scoffing*] This ain't no African war dance, Cap. This is calypso!

CAP: So what? You think I can't dance calypso?

GALAHAD: It need a natural charm and grace, you see. It not like shaking a spear in the air and stamping the ground.

CAP: [*Getting angry*] Listen to you! I suppose all you dance is the whiteman foxtrot and waltz? Them war dances in Africa is where you start from, don't forget, Galahad.

GALAHAD: Don't get racial. I was just making a point. You wait till Daisy come, I will show you... Ah, here she is.

DAISY: [*Coming up*] There was a queue... Hello, Cap.

CAP: Hello luv. Save the next one for me, eh?

GALAHAD: [*Growling*] Lay off my girl, Cap. It have a lot of other birds in the hall.

CAP: But none as nice as Daisy!

DAISY: Just because I came with you, Galahad, doesn't mean I can't dance with who I like.

GALAHAD: [*To Cap*] You keep off, Cap. I warning you... Look how we going to make these motions. Come, Daisy...

Over at the side of the dance hail, Tolroy is arguing with Ma and Tanty...

TOLROY: [*Angrily*] I didn't want to bring the two of you in the first place. This is young people fete.

TANTY: Listen to this boy, Ma! He not too old to take off his trousers and give him some licks!

MA: Hush Tanty! Don't talk so loud let everybody hear you!

TANTY: Well, let me tell you this, Tolroy. You bring me to the dance and you got to have the first set with me.

TOLROY: I going to dance with Jean, who I bring. You and Ma sit down in this corner and keep quiet.

MA: [*Plaintively*] I want a orange squash, Tolroy.

TANTY: I want a big rum! That's what I want, to get me in the mood!

TOLROY: Oh lord, I ain't even had a dance yet and the both of you start to give me trouble! You got to wait until I have a set with Jean... [*Looks around*] Jean? [*She has gone off with somebody*] You see the same blasted thing? While you keep me arguing, somebody take Jean to dance!

TANTY: Good. You could go and get the rum for me in the meantime.

TOLROY: I ain't budging till she come back!

TANTY: That set won't finish now... I will keep she here when it done... Go on, man... and see if they have any ice, I don't see ice in London at all...

MA: [*As Tolroy goes for drinks*] You think the children all right with Agnes and Lewis, Tanty? Is the first time I left them alone, you know.

TANTY: Stop worrying and enjoy yourself, man. As soon as I charge up with a few rums, I going get out there and show them how to shake waist!

MA: The rheumatism not bothering you?

TANTY: What rheumatism? I rub some wintergreen on it last night...

MA: The party remind me of back home, not you?

TANTY: Yes child! You remember Saltfish Hall? They used to have this big bucket of water by the door, and everybody come in from the fields and wash their foot, and go and start jumping up!

MA: I never thought they would of had dance like this in London, with steelband playing... Look, Tolroy coming back...

TOLROY: [*Returning with drinks*] Here. Let this last you the whole night. I didn't come here to spend money on the two of you.

TANTY: [*Rattling ice in the glass*] They have ice, Ma! I ain't had a cold drink since I come London!

TOLROY: [*Impatient*] When the blooming music going to stop? ... I ain't standing up here like a mook, man. I going circulate and meet the boys.

TANTY: You not waiting for Jean? You bring the poor girl to the dance and you lefting she to go and get drunk?

TOLROY: Look, I bring a gin and lime for she... give her when she come...

In the office, Harris is counting the takings. As he counts, there is a knock at the door and Moses comes in...

HARRIS:... five hundred... two and six, five, seven and six, ten...

MOSES: Harris?

HARRIS: Shut the door, old chap. [*Moses shuts it and shuts out the sounds of the music*]... three pounds ten, fifteen...

MOSES: [*Moving to the table*] How it going? Plenty profit?

HARRIS: [*Raking coins into bag*] It looks optimistic, let's say.

MOSES: You got my share put aside? I think I better take it now.

HARRIS: [*Laughing*] Don't be silly! I haven't even checked the takings from the bar!

MOSES: Well, how my fifty looking? It going to double to a hundred... at least?

HARRIS: Oh Moses, you really let me down, old chap. This isn't some illegal deal with Galahad or one of the boys!

MOSES: I just got an evil feeling... a sort of premonition, like, that something might happen...

HARRIS: Rest your fears. Something like what, pray?

MOSES: I don't know... St. Pancras Town Hall might fall down with all that jumping up... The police might make a raid... I don't know... I only know I real bad-lucked ever since I plan and save to go back to Trinidad...

HARRIS: The trouble with you is that misfortune has made you superstitious, Moses... and after all your years in Britain too!

MOSES: Call it what you like. If what happen to me did happen to you, you would of been suspicious too.

HARRIS: Well, not to worry, old thing. Everything is going fine, so far. Forget all that nonsense and have yourself a good time. This will be your last summer fete in London!

MOSES: Yes... well... am, just to please me, Harris, you think I could heft one of those bags that you putting the money in?

HARRIS: What d'you want to do that for?

MOSES: [*Pleading*] Just to please me, Harris... This one here, it look like the most.. .[*Moses lifts the bag off the table with a jingling of silver. It is a real dramatic moment for him. It is as if he is holding the solution to all his problems. He shakes the bag to and fro, listening to the jingling... He speaks direct to the Reporter...*] ... As I hold that money in my hand in that room in St. Pancras Town Hall that night, I really feel great... It was the first time that I ever hold so much money at one time... I forget where I was, I forget Harris and the dance, I forget that dingy basement room in Bayswater, I forget all my sufferings and evil days... I was thinking about how I might be able to open up a little business in Trinidad with all that money... nothing big, perhaps a little parlour in George Street, what selling mauby and rock cake... just something so I could make a little money and don't have to work for anybody... nor have to open the parlour on a Sunday, so I could take the day off and go by the beach and lay down under a coconut tree, and think about the bloody sufferers I left behind me freezing in the old Brit'n.

HARRIS: [*Interrupting the reverie*] That jingle-jangle is like music to your ears, what?

MOSES: [*Back to earth*] About how much in this bag, Harris?

HARRIS: I only made a rough count... Give me, I'll put it in the cash box.

MOSES: You sure that cash box safe? I mean nobody could break into it? You never know with fellars like Big City and Bart around...

HARRIS: Oh, for goodness sake stop worrying, Moses! I am experienced with these affairs...

MOSES: All the same, I would feel a lot better if I could of had my share now.

HARRIS: Do be reasonable, old chap. We haven't begun to take into account the expenses. In a week or two, I will have sorted everything out.

MOSES: A week or two! Why I can't get my money tonight? After the dance? I tell the people at the travel agency I was coming with the full amount tomorrow.

HARRIS: Don't you realise that we have overheads? We've got to pay for the steel band, you know, the boys are not playing for love... We got to pay for the rental of the hall. We've got to pay for the drinks, and the refreshments. We've got to...

MOSES: Yes, yes, all of that is your business, though, I don't want to hear about the politics. I only interested in one thing...

HARRIS: Oh, do be your age, Moses... [*He locks the cash box*]... There. It's safe and sound as if it's in the Bank of England. Let's go and enjoy ourselves... I have some special guests that I haven't had a chance to chat with...

MOSES: [*Grumbling*] Bank of England! Even that ain't secure. Everyday you hear about the devaluation of the pound...

A little later, in the dance hall, Harris is talking to one of his 'important' white guests...

HARRIS:... I'm so glad you were able to come, Mr. Joseph. It lends some dignity to the occasion. And bringing your family along – well, it's a great honour...

MR. JOSEPH: Yes... This is my wife, and my daughter, Miriam...

HARRIS: How do you do? Are you comfortable? Are you enjoying yourselves? Can I get you anything to drink, Mr. Joseph, or would you like to come with me to the bar?

MR. JOSEPH: Quite a noisy crowd at the bar... I'd rather you brought the drinks to the table.

HARRIS: But certainly!

MR. JOSEPH: Soft drinks for the ladies. And I'll have a large scotch.

HARRIS: I shan't be a tick, Mr. Joseph...

At the bar, Harris runs into Galahad and Daisy...

GALAHAD: Hello, Harris! You running round the hall like a blue-fly. Relax and have a drink... You know Daisy?

HARRIS: How d'you do... I can't stay, Galahad. I'm just getting some drinks for my guests.

GALAHAD: What guests?

HARRIS: You remember Mr. Joseph, from the shop. He's brought his family...

GALAHAD: I want to meet him. It look as if he is a sharp businessman. Maybe we could do a few deals together...

HARRIS: Later, Galahad, later. I've got to fly... [*He goes as Cap comes up*]

GALAHAD: Ah Cap! I see you on the floor dancing that last set. You still ain't got the calypso movements, you know. You got to jock your waist and swing your body. Like Big City. Look at him over there...

CAP: Big City look like he out of this world. He has been charging up on some reefers. He and Bart... I thought I might of met Moses here.

GALAHAD: Moses over there with Bob, man... You want a drink?

CAP: Let me buy you and Daisy. You been holding onto the poor girl ever since you come. The usual, Daisy?

DAISY: Yes please, Cap.

GALAHAD: [*Growling to Daisy*] What he mean 'the usual'? You been meeting him behind my back?

DAISY: You don't own me. Just because I allow you to take me out sometimes.

CAP: Relax, Galahad... Have another scotch yourself... Or you feel like dancing?

GALAHAD: If I dance with anybody, it going to be Daisy. I don't trust she alone with you.

CAP: What you think would happen?

GALAHAD: I think you would sneak she out of the dance hall and go home, that's what... so let's get in no confusion here tonight, Cap. Both of we know how we stand.

DAISY: Well I like that! You two discuss me like I was a bit of lost property or something! Haven't I got a say?

CAP: You said your say... the usual, right? Let's have a drink... Who know what the night may yet bring forth?...

There is a loud outcry from the dance floor and the sound of one of the steel band pans falling. Joseph who is with Harris is alarmed...

HARRIS: Good gracious!

MR. JOSEPH: Seems to be some disturbance down there, Harris. What's it about?

HARRIS: [*Disconcerted*] I'm sure it's nothing serious... I'll just nip down and have a look... if you'll please excuse me...

There is a hubbub going on around the band stand as Harris hurries up to the scene, encountering Moses and Bob...

MOSES: Ah, Harris! Big City causing trouble.

HARRIS: What is it, Moses? Anything serious?

MOSES: Well Big City say that he could play pan better than the man in the orchestra, and he went up there and pull the pan out of the man hand while they playing.

HARRIS: Good Lord! I warned you Moses. Couldn't you do anything to stop him?

MOSES: What could I do? Big City and Bart been smoking chargers and both of them in a evil mood... Anyway, it look as if things calm down now...

HARRIS: Thank goodness! I do wish you'd keep your eye on them, Moses. I've got respectable people here tonight, and it would be a bad reflection on us if they misbehave... You sure it's all right?

MOSES: Yes, leave it to me. I'll have a word with Big City...

HARRIS: I'm sorry about this, Bob... the boys get a bit out of hand at times... you know what they're like.

BOB: Oh hell, it was nothing! I was hoping to see some more action!

HARRIS: Yes, well, I'd better get back to Mr. Joseph... [*He goes*]

BOB: Did you see old Harris sweating?

MOSES: Him and his special guests! I heard Big City betting some of the boys that he would go up there and ask Joseph's daughter to have the next dance... I had to cool him off a little, but watch out for him, Bob, them chargers he been smoking have him wild tonight. If you notice he up to anything, give me a shout.

BOB: Like hell! I want to see him doing a calypso with her... She's got on an evening dress too! D'you think he will?

MOSES: The night is young: anything could happen. But try to help me to preserve the peace, Bob. I got money invested in this fete.

BOB: You were saying you actually held some of the takings in your hand?

MOSES: Yes, I went into the office to make sure all this wasn't no dream. But it safe and sound... like in the Bank of England... Come let's go have a drink...

They are on their way to the bar when Tanty calls out.

TANTY: Moses! You still in London, boy? I thought you did leave for home long ago!

MOSES: I still have a few things to tend to, Tanty.

TANTY: Well come and talk a little with me and Ma. Bring your friend, too...

BOB: [*In an undertone to Moses*] I can think of a better way to pass time... Meet me at the bar... [*Bob goes*]

MOSES: I can't stay, Tanty, I was just going to have a drink with my friend.

TANTY: Don't be selfish like Tolroy! He left me and Ma sit down in this corner and we ain't seen him since. Come tell me your troubles, son... I thought you was in Trinidad by now!

MOSES: Yes... Well... I'm leaving. In a few days.

TANTY: At last, eh, at last! You hear that, Ma? Moses lefting England!

MA: I hear... I think I going look for Tolroy, I tired sit down here.

TANTY: Good idea... Look by the bar, he sure to be drunkening himself! [*Ma goes*]

MOSES: Look ,Tanty, my friend waiting on me.

TANTY: Sit down in Ma chair, son... I hear you had so much trouble! Tolroy was telling me... but since he left the factory and working with the Transport people-them, he say he ain't seen you, and you must of gone home... How you like Tolroy in conductor uniform? He look good, eh?

MOSES: Yeah...

TANTY: You should of done conductor work too, Moses. You would of got more money than that stupid factory in Kensal Rise... You been dancing? This is young people fete, you know! You got to enjoy yourself!

MOSES: I had a set or two.

TANTY: [*Eagerly*] You got the next set book?

MOSES: I just dance when I feel like it.

TANTY: Well book the next set with me, eh?

MOSES: Not that one, the one after that, all right?

TANTY: Up to now I ain't jump up, and is my first dance in London... and I only had one little rum from that mingy Tolroy.

MOSES: [*Seeking escape*] You want a drink?

TANTY: A large one, Moses! It would just put me right!

MOSES: Good. I'll get one for you... or send it by Tolroy...

TANTY: I could come to the bar!

MOSES: [*As she rises*] No, no, Tanty! You just sit nice and quiet there, and look at all our country people having a good time.

Moses hurries to the bar, where he meets Bob and Tolroy...

BOB: Back already?

MOSES: Oh lord! I barely manage to escape Tanty! [*Spots Tolroy*] Aye, Tolroy! Tanty want a drink!

TOLROY: I just send something over by Bart.

MOSES: Why you bring them two old people to the dance?

TOLROY: I didn't bring them, man. They dress up and follow me!

BOB: What're you grumbling about, Moses? The more the merrier, as far as your investment is concerned!

TOLROY: What investment?

MOSES: Don't tell him anything, Bob, until I on the boat, and it cast off from Plymouth or Southampton, or whatever port.

TOLROY: [*This is enough for him: he knows*] I have a idea, Bob.

BOB: Good. Hoard it, and look after it carefully. You mightn't get another!

TOLROY: I going to get Cap to start up a stay-in-Brit'n movement for Moses. That is what he want we to do. Because, believe you me, Bob, the day Moses left these shores, I will be Chief Executive of London Transport instead of conductor on a number 18 bus...

Harris is still talking to Joseph...

MR. JOSEPH: What was all that about, Harris?

HARRIS: Nothing, nothing at all, Mr. Joseph. Just a little exuberance.

MR. JOSEPH: Sit down Harris. My family is absent... for the moment... These things that you organise for the immigrants... good business?

HARRIS: It's just a sort of sideline with me, actually.

MR. JOSEPH: Seems a paying one, judging from the crowd here tonight... maybe we could do something together sometime, eh? As you know, I've got a finger in many pies...

HARRIS: [*Reluctant to share with anybody*] I don't think it's a good idea to become too involved in the social activities of my people, Mr. Joseph. Most of them know me, and, actually...

MR. JOSEPH: Nonsense. Anything that makes money is my business. I sell them clothes and other household items, don't I? You work for me yourself!

HARRIS: Are you suggesting a partnership?

MR. JOSEPH: You can call it that if you like... though I'm not sure of you, Harris. You don't seem to have enough push.

HARRIS: [*Stiffly*] You wouldn't get another immigrant who gets on so well with the English people as I do, Mr. Joseph. Why, I have friends in high circ...

MR. JOSEPH: I know, I know, don't forget I employed you... That chap who was supposed to go away, why's he still around?

HARRIS: You mean Moses?

MR. JOSEPH: No no! Some historical name... Galahad?

HARRIS: Galahad isn't leaving. Moses is the one who is planning a departure from the shores of...

MR. JOSEPH: Yes, Galahad... that the chap who bought that record player, right? Where does he work?

HARRIS: I don't know for sure... but I can easily find out for you... I believe he left the factory where he was employed... To the best of my knowledge he is just knocking about.

MR. JOSEPH: [*Thoughtfully*] H'mm... I'd like to see him...

HARRIS: No sooner said than done, Mr. Joseph!

MR. JOSEPH: Eh?

HARRIS: Excuse me, for a moment there I slipped into the vernacular... I shall have him here in a minute, if you'll excuse me.

MR. JOSEPH: And bring me back another large scotch, Harris, with lots of ice...

HARRIS: Certainly, Mr. Joseph...

Harris goes to the bar, where he finds Galahad and Daisy...

GALAHAD: Ah! Here is Mr. Harris himself, sweating like a donkey... Harris! You not keeping order in the hall, man! These disturbances don't show you in a good light.

HARRIS: Galahad, Mr. Joseph wants to see you.

GALAHAD: I don't know any Mr. Joseph.

HARRIS: My boss, man, who owns the shop on Portobello Road.

GALAHAD: Oh! Wants to talk business, eh?

HARRIS: I don't know, but you will be doing me a great favour by seeing him. He is one of my special guests...

GALAHAD: Sure, sure... Wait here for me, Daisy, at the bar.

DAISY: This is a dance, Galahad. I don't intend to sit on a stool all night!

GALAHAD: [*Leaving*] I won't be long... You wait right here... you coming, Harris?

HARRIS: Yes, I'll just get this drink for Mr. Joseph.

As Galahad and Harris leave the bar, Cap moves in on Daisy...

CAP: There you are, Daisy, my luv. These boys are always thinking of money.

DAISY: I'm glad he's gone! He's too possessive for my liking! Expects me to wait around on his beck and call!

CAP: Have another gin and lime... You and me ain't had a chance to talk! ... You like my national costume?

DAISY: It's smashing! Is that what you wear as a chieftain?

CAP: Yes. I thought you would like it... I got the other one, too.

DAISY: Other one?

CAP: I mean the one that the Queen of the tribes wear... It might just fit you, Daisy!

DAISY: Oh! I must try it on next time I come.

CAP: No time like tonight... I mean it have fetes like this in London all the time. It's only a dance. We could leave a bit early...

DAISY: You know how jealous Galahad is... We still have three hours to go!

CAP: Let's have a dance in the meantime, luv. Why we sitting around when nice music playing? [*They dance*]

There is more shouting and scandalous laughter from the dance floor suggesting that the fete is getting a little out of hand. A worried and sweating Harris is looking for, and finds, Bob and Moses sitting a set out in a corner. Everybody except Harris is well away with drinks...

HARRIS: Moses! I am so glad I found you!

MOSES: Why? What happen?

HARRIS: [*He is slipping more and more into dialect in his anxiety*] I don't like how it's going, man. Can't you stop Big City from dancing so... so... sexy? And Bart! Look at him, trying to balance a bottle of rum on his head in that corner!

BOB: This is great, Harris! I've been to some little do's in my time, but man, this is great! Great!

MOSES: What you expect me to do, Harris?

HARRIS: You've invested, you know. I don't want things to get out of hand. Can't you have a word with Big City? He would listen to you quicker than me... actually.

MOSES: All I want is my hundred pounds for the fifty that I invest, and I will leave the hall like a bullet...

HARRIS: [*Appealing*] Bob! Moses been drinking. Can I rely on you?

BOB: Anytime, Harris, anytime!

HARRIS: My main concern is towards the end... you know, when we play the National Anthem? These boys have a habit of dancing to it, actually...

BOB: Dancing to the National Anthem?

HARRIS: They've done it before... I've got special guests, Bob. Moses doesn't understand. Think of the impression it will give to the English people who are present here tonight...

BOB: You leave everything to me, Harris. I will impress the English people like they've never been impressed before!

HARRIS: [*Anxiously*] *You* haven't been drinking too?

BOB: I shall attend to things. How does Moses put it? 'Matters fixed'.

HARRIS: I hope so, Bob, I earnestly hope so... I've got to get back and see what is so interesting about Galahad... he and Mr. Joseph have been having what amounts to a business conference...

Harris is on his way when Tanty spots him and calls out...

TANTY: Mr. Harris!

HARRIS: I can't stop now...

TANTY: MR. HARRIS!

HARRIS: Well what is it? Please be quick!

TANTY: I know you, though you mightn't know me!

HARRIS: I have many friends...

TANTY: Come on then! You passing by the ladies? I dying to have a set! The steel band music have my feet tapping!

HARRIS: Yes, of course... well...

TANTY: You can't leave me sitting like a poor-me-one in this corner!

HARRIS: Of course not, miss, Mrs.?

TANTY: I's Tolroy Tanty! You know Tolroy?

HARRIS: I'll be back in a tick, Mrs. Tolroy... I mean, Tanty.

TANTY: Oh no you wouldn't... that's what all the boys been saying to me... Even Ma dancing! Let we show them how to dance a calypso!

HARRIS: [*Taking breath*] Really, Mrs... Tanty, I am honoured, but...

TANTY: [*Getting up*] No buts! You don't respect your elders? If you can't dance calypso I will teach you...

MOSES: [*Addressing the reporter direct*] ... so that night in St. Pancras

78

Town Hall, everything was going roses... I didn't mind how worried Harris was, because, as you know, he always playing la-de-da, and me and the other boys had a good laugh when we see Tanty catch hold of him and start to dance, and poor Harris hands could barely cover Tanty waist... yes, it was going good. In fact, so good, that I begin to get a little homesick for Brit'n, because we like to show the English people how we could really enjoy weselves, and that night was a good example. I mean, there was Big City, going to town on the dance hall... and old Bart. The two of them ain't miss a set that night, they was dancing all the time... even my good friend Bob, who was the only English friend I make in Brit'n, was dancing, because every time I pick up a thing, I put she on to Bob... I say it already and I will say it again, that I would rather do him a favour than any of those reprobates who pretend to be my friends... Well, at last I had a word with Big City, he come to me and say that he was tired dancing with all the chicks standing around, that he was going to ask one of Harris special guests to honour him with a set. I try to put him off, because he was high, but it turn out that he had a bet with the boys that he could do it. Anyway, the way how calamity happen that night, I not sure which was the cause, if it was that, as Big City went and pull Mr. Joseph daughter from the table and start to dance and jerk his waist, or if is because Cap was holding Daisy too tight, and Galahad get vex. But all of a sudden, as if pandemonium burst loose in St. Pancras Town Hall...

Back to the dance... Commotion everywhere. Big City is in trouble with Mr. Joseph; Galahad is fighting with Cap over Daisy; Tanty is yelling for a partner to dance; bottles are broken; there are screams; a rush for the exit...

FIRST VOICE: God! Send for the police!

SECOND VOICE: I know this would of happen! OUR PEOPLE could never organise!

THIRD VOICE: I getting out of here!

FOURTH VOICE: The fete just start! I want my money back! Where Harris?

FIFTH VOICE: [*English*] Yeah, money back... bloody immigrants always end up in confusion...

Later at the entrance, Harris is paying back disappointed people...

HARRIS: I'm so sorry... Here you are... I'll let you know where the next venue is... Help me Moses! I can't cope with everything!

MOSES: Yes... am... well, you sure you pay to come in? I recognise you, you know. You from Brixton!

HARRIS: Just give them their money back, Moses! Don't argue.

VOICE: It matter where I come from? I want my money back!

HARRIS: Of course... [*Mr. Joseph is coming out with his family*] Mr. Joseph! I have to render my utmost apologies.

MR. JOSEPH: Never mind, Harris. You're fired.

HARRIS: Fired?

MR. JOSEPH: Yes... Your friend Galahad will tell you. No, no, I don't want my money back! We were going to leave early anyway.

TANTY: [*Shrilly*] What *commess* here tonight, Moses!

MOSES: Yes, Tanty, but just pass along, you blocking the crowd.

TANTY: [*Loudly*] Well I got this to say, and I don't care who hear it! If this is the way you all behave in the white man country, I for one going to wash my hands from ever coming to any dance!

TOLROY: [*Behind Tanty*] Yeah, yeah... I bring in four chicks with me, Moses, if you remember...

MOSES: All you getting back is what you pay to come in.

HARRIS: [*Desperately*] Get Bob to help, man Moses! The two of we can't cope with the... exodus...

Later, Moses, Bob, Harris, Galahad and Daisy are in the office. They are having a sad postmortem on the affair. A worried Harris paces to and fro...

MOSES: Stop pacing up and down like a lion a cage, Harris.

HARRIS: I've got to think, Moses, I've got to think!

BOB: What about, Harris? It's happened already, hasn't it?

HARRIS: [*Mournfully*] True enough, Bob. But the future! I've been giving these social occasions for years, and why did it have to come to a head tonight? There has never been trouble before... Anyway, not enough for the participants to demand their money back!

GALAHAD: [*Lazily, lolling on the floor with Daisy in his arms, unconcerned about Moses's and Harris's misfortune*] If you ask me, Harris, I will

80

tell you that the fete was doom when Moses put a hand in it. You should of ask me to help.

MOSES: All I do is invest fifty pounds! I had nothing to do with the arrangements. Harris should of had police here to take care of any... any...

BOB: Misdemeanours, Moses. Look boys, I'm fresh. I went to the gents and washed my face... and whatever happens, I want to see my mate Moses right... How did the whole thing happen, anyway?

DAISY: [*After a pause*] Well! I shouldn't be here in the first place, but for Galahad dragging me into the office.

GALAHAD: [*Growling*] Keep out of it! You cause enough trouble!

HARRIS: [*Stops pacing*] Ah! Though it is of little value at this stage, I would like to know, for future performances, what led to this catastrophe, if I ever live it down.

MOSES: Well!

HARRIS: I would like Daisy to speak, do you mind?

DAISY: Well honestly Harris! You had certain people here who are only fit for a drunken party in the East End! I mean like Big City.

GALAHAD: You know Big City?

DAISY: I don't, but while I was alone for a moment, he suggested...

HARRIS: [*Hastily*] We don't want to go into the terrible details! Have you any idea what started off this... this... disaster?

BOB: It's no use asking Daisy, Harris. I know what happened.

HARRIS: Well?

BOB: It started off with Big City being challenged to dance with your Mr. Joseph's daughter.

HARRIS: I expected something like that!

BOB: But there was also trouble between Cap and Galahad, over Daisy.

MOSES: I don't see the use of this postmortem. What happen, happen. All my money gone down the drain! [*He is almost in tears*]

HARRIS: I would like to clarify the position, Moses, if you do not mind... You were saying, Bob?

BOB: Hell! What more d'you want to know? There was confusion when Big City took Joseph's daughter to the dance floor, Galahad here caught Cap dancing with Daisy... and a fight broke out, that's all.

HARRIS: If *you* started it, Galahad, I will sue you!

GALAHAD: Before you do that, you better consider. Mr. Joseph offer me your job. He say he could use a good man.

HARRIS: So that is what you were talking about behind my back! I should have known!

MOSES: [*Groaning*] Lord, lord... What all this about? What we going to do now? All the money gone back to the people who come in, and I, Moses Aloetta Esquire, invest in the dance! You boys don't seem to realise what happen to me here tonight! My plans have gone awry! Everything turn old mask, as the saying goes!

DAISY: [*Aside to Galahad*] What does he mean?

GALAHAD: He means he still here in England, he can't move an inch. [*Louder*] I suggest we tackle the bar and see what remaining. I always like to mop up after my deals.

BOB: In case you leave fingerprints, eh?

GALAHAD: You *know*, Bob! Go and see what left in the bar. We might raise a few drinks, for consolation.

BOB: [*Going*] I could do with a beer, if anything's left. [*Bob goes*]

MOSES: [*After a pause*] So what happen now, Harris? To my investment in the dance?

HARRIS: You can see, old chap... the situation has got out of hand. I hardly know where I stand myself!

MOSES: You mean that I back where I started from!

HARRIS: Well! Not exactly. Next summer...

MOSES: [*Angrily*] Don't tell me nothing 'bout next summer, man! I fix up to leave England tomorrow! I got all my things packed.

HARRIS: Let's be reasonable about this, Moses. There is so much to take into consideration. We seem to have come across a bad patch, at the moment, but we've got to take the rough with the smooth.

MOSES: Come out flat and let me know where I stand, man! What about the takings from the bar? And all that food. Pig foot and peas and rice and chicken and ham and...

BOB: [*Coming back, interrupting*] Here we are, boys. All that's left. A crate of beer, and a few sad sandwiches, rather English... cucumber and tomatoes.

HARRIS: I should have known! I warned you to keep an eye on the bar, Moses. They must have... er... rustled the bar, and the food.

BOB: [*Trying to brighten things up*] Well, no use crying after spilt milk, eh? Might as well make use of this... Beer, Moses?

MOSES: Beer! You think that would console me? I lose my passage money, man!

GALAHAD: I taking over from Harris in future, Moses. Even the job in the shop Mr. Joseph say I could have, after I offer him a cigar... I will fix you up in a jiffy. We even have travel agent connections, charter flights, and that sort of thing. You could go home by plane instead of boat.

DAISY: I'm disgusted with all this! Let's go Galahad. There's no need to keep on here. You boys haven't the faintest clue. All this talk, and talk...

MOSES: Well and good for you, Daisy. I am the one lose the most here tonight.

BOB: Come on! Who's for a beer? Daisy, pass around the sandwiches...

REPORTER: Well! It sounds as if you nearly made it that time, Moses!

MOSES: That fete at St. Pancras Town Hall set me back a long time. It was always touch and go until, in the end, I had was to give up the idea. Until now, that is...

REPORTER: So you *still* want to go back? After all that's happened? Surely things must have changed for you since those days! With the Immigration Bill...

MOSES: Sure they change! But for better or worse, that's the question...

PART FIVE: CAP CAPTURES A BIRD

REPORTER: What a pity, Moses, that things had to get out of hand at that dance of Harris's...

MOSES: Yes. That was the first and last time I invest. We got a saying you know, that 'Every day not Sunday', or to put it another way, 'After one time is another'.

REPORTER: What does that mean, exactly?

MOSES: All that feting and skylarking in the summer wasn't going to last. In fact, I remember it was shortly after that frolic at St. Pancras... in which I lost the money I had save to return to Trinidad...

REPORTER: Yes! You must be the most unfortunate man in London, Moses.

MOSES: You think all them experiences I been telling you about is bad luck? Let me tell you about the bitter times that follow. It was as if the vengeance of the gods fall on all the boys in Londontown. Fellars losing their jobs left right and centre and can't get nothing to do and had was to go on the dole. Any time you wanted to see one of the boys – you know where to look – the employment exchange. We used to line up there every Thursday and ask one another, 'Any change?' And back came the answer, 'No change.' Of the set of us, Tolroy was the only one plodding steady with London Transport. Harris was as if failure only spur him onto higher realms of speculation and fantasy in his dream world. Even Cap, who in the roughest times would be able to haul out a pack of cigarettes and pass it around, was only dreaming about this money they was going to send for him from Nigeria. And Galahad was picking up odds and ends from the shady Mr. Joseph, and aspiring to the big times. But while this depression was hitting the boys hard, lots of things was changing in the old Brit'n. The Government start to talk about a Immigration Bill to shut the door on hustlers from the islands, and all over the country, black people was beginning to organise themselves, lest they get lost or pushed aside in the general scramble. One morning I was talking upstairs with Bob about how the situation was getting desperate...

Bob's room in Bayswater...

BOB: ...I think you'll manage, Moses. After all, you have been in worse jams than this.

MOSES: What worse jams than for a man to lose his job? I tell you, Bob, everything been against me from the day I decide to go back to Trinidad. And now, to crown it all, I got a chance to move out of the basement and take your room, and I can't!

BOB: You can use it for the rest of my lease, which I've paid up already. Don't you want to shift from that cold, damp room, with a leaking skylight! My God, I don't know how you've stood it all these years. This is for free, man! You can live without paying rent for a month.

MOSES: I going to miss you, Bob... You know, is a funny thing, I never thought you would of got married.

BOB: Yeah... but I got to settle some time... You want to meet her, Moses.

MOSES: [*Vaguely*] Yes... Sometime.

BOB: No, come on, I'm serious... How about a drink in the pub this evening? I'll bring her along.

MOSES: We'll see...

BOB: I know what that means... You won't turn up.

MOSES: Well let's face it, Bob. I been years in this country, and I was never asked by any of the English blokes I know to come and see them. They all right at work, and if you meet them in the pub, but after that they don't know you.

BOB: What are you trying so hard to say?

MOSES: That when you move from Bayswater and get married, you and me might never meet again, except by accident.

BOB: You think I'd just blow and forget you, and that meal you've always been promising to cook me? When Maureen and me get settled in that flat in Hampstead, you're going to come one evening and do it.

MOSES: Hampstead is a posh area. It don't have many of US up there.

BOB: So what's all this sudden talk about then? You're starting to sound like Cap and all that political nonsense he's mixed up in. I've always treated you like anybody else. You never hear me sounding off on racial issues, mate.

MOSES: I know, Bob, that's why you and me get on so well.

BOB: Well what's all this, then?

MOSES: Just suppose, Bob, we only supposing... that Maureen don't like coloured people? Suppose I come in that pub this evening, and she only talk to me for your sake?

BOB: You haven't even met her and you draw conclusions!

MOSES: You're the one marrieding, not me. *My* conclusions not important...

BOB: Sure they are! But don't form them in advance! I don't want you to go back to Trinidad and say that the only English bloke you knew turned out to be a bastard in the end! Or that he was all right, but his wife was different!

MOSES: I glad you remind me of my departure... It would be nice to live up here instead of the basement, even for a few weeks.

BOB: You'll take the room, then?

MOSES: Yes... and thanks a lot, Bob.

BOB: You got a month free, right? Don't let the bloody Polish landlord tell you otherwise... And another thing. I been asking at the Town Hall about when I leave this job next week. They'll need a man... You don't mind portering, do you?

MOSES: You know I would do anything, Bob! I near enough to my passage money.

BOB: There you are. I got you a new room, and I got you prospects of a job... you're happy?

MOSES: You mean I could move up here right away?

BOB: Sure. I just got to take one or two things that I left behind... smashing flat in Hampstead, boy. Got our own little kitchen. No more gas rings for yours truly... and Maureen to do the cooking...

MOSES: I better start shifting my things up – I'm going to feel strange, coming through the front door instead of going down to the basement!

BOB: I'll see you in the pub this evening around seven?

MOSES: All right, Bob. As long as you buying the drinks. Don't forget I'm on the dole.

BOB: I'll just nip up and see the landlord and make it clear that you're moving in for the rest of the lease...

Later... Moses comes into Bob's old room, panting, carrying an armchair from his basement. It has a sentimental value...

MOSES: ...settle there, armchair... to give you up would be like giving up all my years in the Water. Everyone of the boys sit in you. People come and go and sleep in you, and sit on your arms... But at last you have a decent room to live in... you promoted upstairs. You just settle down there, and learn to live in better surroundings... [*There is a knock on the door*] Who the hell can that be? [*He goes out to the door and brings back Galahad*].

GALAHAD: Oh! I thought you might be up here, after I try the basement... Where Bob?

MOSES: Bob ain't here, and I don't want to see you Galahad... I just moving in.

GALAHAD: I don't forget *my* friends!

MOSES: Friends... huh! You *got* any friends?

GALAHAD: I just came because I hear Bob moving out for Hampstead, and I put two and two together and make five, figuring out that, as you and Bob such good friends, you may be promoting to Bob's room, which you are! But you got a problem here, moving from basement to first floor... there's a difference you know. Right away I could spot it.

MOSES: Spot what?

GALAHAD: The difference. You can't move that basement... er, equipment, up to this room on the first floor! Look at your things against what Bob had here before... no comparison at all!

MOSES: You just leave me alone to get on with my shifting.

GALAHAD: But that old armchair, Moses! Surely you don't mean to keep that in your new room?

MOSES: You don't remember that you sleep in it your first night in Londontown? This armchair remind me of all the reprobates and layabouts that sit down in it. I remember one night Cap hustle in from a dreadful fall of snow, and curl up there and sleep like a baby...

GALAHAD: Give you two quid for it, Moses? Cash?

MOSES: [*Reacting to this unexpected offer*] You said two quid for this old chair? I wanted to get rid of it.

GALAHAD: I was just quoting a bargaining figure... let's have a look...
[*Approaches chair and examines* it] Ummm... It got a lot of coffee
and tea stains...

MOSES: That's where you, and the boys, spill your drinks. Otherwise
I keep it clean. That chair is my own property, that I bought to
rest myself in... When it come to selling it, I got to think
different.

GALAHAD: I'm in the trade, Moses. You can't pull a fast one on me.

MOSES: You mean the great Galahad reduce to a rag and bone man?

GALAHAD: Only for the time being. As soon as I come up with a big
idea to Mr. Joseph, he going to consider me for better things.
The trouble with Harris was he never come up with any ideas,
you see, that's why Mr. Joseph put me in his place... but things
so hard at the moment, Moses, as you know... it difficult to
make a living. I mean, even you could do with a couple of quid,
couldn't you?

MOSES: Agreed. Except that I don't trust you... I wouldn't let you move
the armchair unless you wave that two pounds in my face... and
add a ten-shilling note, to make it look as if you really serious.

GALAHAD: [*Taking out money*] Sold then, for two ten. You hold me
this time, boy Moses, but I happen to know that Cap is in need
for some relaxation, while he meditates on the allowances he
awaits from Nigeria, and the racial problems of Great Britain.

MOSES: [*Hesitant*] If you give me two pounds, ten...

GALAHAD: [*Pushing money on Moses*] Here... Fifty bob.

MOSES: This is the first time I *got* money from you! Maybe something special about this chair... I always reading about these
Americans coming over to buy antique furniture.

GALAHAD: All right. Give me back my money, and flog that tea-
stained, torn-up dilapidated chair that you get from some
second-hand shop...

MOSES: [*Quickly*] Okay, it's yours, Galahad. But somehow I feel as
if you got the better of me.

GALAHAD: [*Laughs*] Huh! I got the problem of selling it to Cap or
some other customer, while you sit back and laugh with two
pounds ten in your hand... I got the van outside. You going to
help me take it away?

MOSES: As soon as I fold this money and put it in my pocket... You
going to Cap, first?

GALAHAD: I might as well, seeing that I'm in the Water... [*They carry the chair to the door*]... There... I could manage it to the van...

> Later, Cap's room. The bell rings and Cap looks down from the attic window and shouts...

CAP: [*Uncertain who it is*] Who's that?

GALAHAD: [*Shouting up*] Aye, Cap! It's Galahad!

CAP: Hold on, boy! I throw the key!... You got it?

GALAHAD: Yes... [*Shortly there is the sound of Galahad climbing the stairs and then he enters the room... Gasping*] You halfway to hell boy!

CAP: Yes, bo. This is my cabin in the sky. Come in.

GALAHAD: I got that armchair downstairs in the van, man. The short one you said you were interested in!

CAP: [*Shutting the door*] Never mind that for the moment... You got a fag, Galahad? I just happen to run out...

GALAHAD: Yeah... sure [*Offers a cigarette, and they light up*].

CAP: [*Inhaling deeply*] Ah, bo! ... when you get a smoke, it kill your hunger... You didn't happen to bring anything to eat?

GALAHAD: It ain't lunch yet, man!

CAP: You mean lunchtime yesterday or today? Boy, I am having it rough... I'm busy making notes for the party, collecting data for the march on Sunday.

GALAHAD: I will turn up and swell the ranks... What about a cup of tea? It cold outside, you know.

CAP: I couldn't even raise that, bo. To tell you the truth, what I was doing when the bell ring was laying down on the bed here, thinking of things like chop suey, or chicken biriani, and other English specialities

GALAHAD: You really in a bad way. But I in the same boat. I got to sell that armchair, else I lose my job with Mr. Joseph.

CAP: I thought you were in the big times, not selling second-hand furniture.

GALAHAD: It all takes a little time... today rag and bone, tomorrow... who knows?

CAP: You got to excuse me while I lay down, I find if you conserve you energy, you don't feel so hungry... [*He lies back on the bed*]... This is how I was just before you came, thinking about how I nearly catch one of them pigeons in the park yesterday.

GALAHAD: What pigeons?

CAP: In the park, man. They only flying about the place and not serving any useful purpose. They congregate near the Bayswater Road, where them old geezers feed them with bread and biscuits. I try to snatch one, but as luck would have it, same time a old woman was walking her dog nearby, and she see me. You could imagine! She bawl for murder, and I had was to drop the pigeon and make races!

GALAHAD: [*Laughing*] I remember in Trinidad my father used to catch them and put them in a paper bag and send them home, and we have pigeon stew for the next day!

CAP: Don't talk about food I beg you. Is only aggravating my hunger. It even have sea gulls what come up from the Thames, and roost in Londontown, on all them ledges on them tall buildings. I even see them fly by this window up here in the attic... [*A thought strikes him...*] Aye! Suppose it have some by the ledge outside?

GALAHAD: You mean here. By your window?

CAP: Yes. [*He is agitated now*] Suppose it have meat roosting here all the time while I starving? I seen them passing while I lay down here on the bed, and I never thought of it before! [*He looks up to the skylight*] There! You seen that! One just pass! And as if it settling on the ledge, too, the way it was flapping the wings.

GALAHAD: You best had make sure. Open the window and have a look.

Cap opens the window and cranes his neck out left and right... he is full of hunger and excited now...

CAP: Yes Galahad! It got six fat ones! Birds on this attic ledge all the time! We could set a trap and catch one!

GALAHAD: Don't make so much noise, you will frighten them. What sort of trap?

CAP: [*Moving from the window*] A little string... you make a loop in it and then you tug, and bam! you got it... We got to do this carefully, Galahad. Come on and help me... Get the string... Look in that corner...

GALAHAD: You got any bread?

CAP: Bread! What for?

GALAHAD: Well you got to put bait. Them birds won't come unless you put some sort of bait! You must of got a piece of stale bread somewhere, man.

CAP: Look near the stove, you might see some crumbs... I got the trap fix good.

GALAHAD: Let me see... Man! That's not the way we do it in Trinidad when we want to catch a bird! You should put something to fall right on top of him, bam! As he touch the bread.

CAP: Bo, oh, my trap is to get him *inside*. Once we got him here, we won't have any problem.

GALAHAD: We don't do it like that in Trinidad...

CAP: Just let me do it my way, bo?

GALAHAD: Okay, set your trap.

He leans out of the window setting the trap. There is a pause as they wait...

CAP: [*In a whisper*] You seen that fellar? He almost get in the loop!

GALAHAD: Just get the bird inside the room, man... The next one come, you just make a snatch...

CAP: I got it...!

GALAHAD: Get it inside quick!

CAP: I got it inside. It get away! Shut the window!

GALAHAD: [*Shutting the window*] Where it gone?

The bird hovers about, cawing at them... [In staging this scene the bird could either exist as a stage prop suspended on wire above the set, or be created through Cap's and Galahad's responses to it]

CAP: We got to catch it, Galahad!

GALAHAD: Drive it off the cupboard!

There is a big attempt to catch the bird, which always manages to stay one step ahead of Cap's and Galahad's vain lunges after it...

CAP: Watch it Galahad!

GALAHAD: I nearly got it... Over by you!

CAP: Yes, it only fluttering around now... Coo... coo... coo!

GALAHAD: You putting it off! Is not a pigeon, is a sea gull!

CAP: Well, quee, quee, quee!... Catch it off the table!

GALAHAD: Aps! I miss it! I only got a feather! It gone on the bed!

CAP: Grab it quick, man.

GALAHAD: [*Pausing for breath*] Look, wait a minute, We got to plan this properly. We ain't getting no place.

CAP: Is two big men against a little sea gull, man. We must catch it!

GALAHAD: That's what I mean... Now look. You see it there in the corner? Right. Get the blanket off the bed. Do it easy, don't frighten him... That's right... Now come over here and stand up... I going to drive him out of the corner, and the moment he fly up, you throw the blanket over him. You got the idea?

CAP: Yes... I ready now. Hurry up quick!

GALAHAD: [*Getting to the corner slowly*] Shoo! shoo, bird, shoo!

The sea gull flutters up. Cap makes a wild dive with the blanket and covers it. He capsizes the small table in his excitement. A dirty plate, cup and saucer crash and break on the floor...

CAP: [*Breathing hard*] I got him, I got him!

There is a furious pounding on the door, and the shrill voice of the landlady outside...

LANDLADY: Mr. Cap! What's happening in there?

GALAHAD: [*In a frightened voice*] Who is that?

CAP: Oh lord, is the landlady! ... [*Loudly*] It's nothing, Mrs. Watson!

LANDLADY: What's all the noise? Open up this door at once!

CAP: [*Loud whisper*] What we going to do?

GALAHAD: Make some excuse quick, man!

CAP: [*Loudly*] I can't, Mrs. Watson. I changing my clothes!

LANDLADY: I don't believe you! Something is going on... [*She uses her key to open the door, looks in and slowly takes in the disorderly state of the room...*] What on earth do you think you're doing? Who is this man? The room is in a shambles!

CAP: [*Weakly*] Just a friend...

LANDLADY: And look at my broken crockery! Have you been fighting?

GALAHAD: No lady... let me explain...

LANDLADY: [*Snapping*] I don't want to hear you! You'll have to go, Mr. Cap, I... [*Sees the blanket on the floor*] What's my blanket doing on the floor? And... what's under it?

CAP: [*Quickly*] It's nothing... I was just tidying up...

LANDLADY: [*Insistent*] There is something moving there... [*She moves into the room and picks up the blanket. The sea gull flutters away and alights on the cupboard.*] ... Good gracious me! It's a bird!

CAP: Yes... Well, you see...

LANDLADY: How did it get in here? The poor thing!

CAP: That's just it, you see... I had the window open for a little fresh air... and it come inside. Ain't that so, Galahad?

GALAHAD: Er... yes. We was just sitting here at the table talking peacefully, when it fly inside...

CAP: And we was trying to catch it to put it outside again... that's why all the noise was making, you see...

LANDLADY: The poor thing! How do you expect it to get out with the window shut? [*She opens the window*] ... There. Now shoo it away gently from the cupboard...

CAP: Am... you can go now, Mrs. Watson, we will look after it and see that it gets out...

LANDLADY: I don't want it in my room! Come on, there's a cold draught from the window... Let your friend help.

CAP: [*Half-heartedly*] Shoo, pigeon, shoo.

GALAHAD: [*Trying to get it behind the cupboard, if anything*] I'll just wave my arms here...

LANDLADY: Don't be silly! Get on the other side... both of you! You're standing in front and crowding the poor creature back into the room... That's better.

CAP: This might take some time... We don't want to stop you from your housework, Mrs. Watson.

LANDLADY: My mind wouldn't be easy until I see it free... Move out of the way, you two... You haven't the faintest idea how to treat dumb creatures... Here, birdie... here... [*She makes some cooing noises and gets the bird out and shuts the window*] ... There... What a state you've got the room in! You'll have to pay for the broken plate and cup you know... As a matter of fact, I wanted a word with you, Mr. Cap.

CAP: Well... later, I'll come down.

LANDLADY: I don't mind talking in front of your friend... You haven't budged from this room for days, and you owe me two weeks' rent.

CAP: As soon as I get my allowance from Nigeria...

LANDLADY: I've heard enough about that precious allowance. If you don't square up by the ending of the week, I'm afraid I'll have to take drastic steps...

We move back to Moses, in his narrative voice...

MOSES: [*With a chuckle*] That was like adding insult to injury for poor Cap! Of course, he himself never say anything about that sea gull... It was Galahad who give the boys the ballad, but Cap confess to me afterwards how he used to dream about birds flying about the room, and wake up to find himself making some wild snatch in the air, hopeful for a pigeon stew! But I could tell you that I had enough worries of my own than to bother about what happening with the other boys... I mean, is funny the way how things happen. Here I was in this new room upstairs, living in a decent place for the first time, but I didn't have no job! As things was, any minute I would have to dig into that sweat-and-blood money that I had save up for my trip home. Even the idea of that was like a dream now, as if it could never happen. Ah well! I was getting ready to go to the pub and meet Bob and his gracious lady, when who should knock but the great Harris...

HARRIS: [*Coming into the room*] ...My dear Moses! I wanted to be the very first to congratulate you.

MOSES: For what?

HARRIS: Why, for your new digs! What a change from that dingy basement room, eh!

MOSES: Lord! A man just move up today, and already everybody in Londontown know about it!

HARRIS: [*Looking around*] This is absolutely super! At last you'd be able to entertain some decent folk... How is dear Bob, by the way? I haven't seen him for ages.

MOSES: I going to meet him now, in the pub. You know he getting married?

HARRIS: Is he? That's wonderful news, wonderful. It's the best thing to do really. There's no future in drifting around. I myself have been contemplating a life of bliss with some goodly woman...

MOSES: [*Sarcastic*] Is that so? How you going to support a wife?

HARRIS: My dear fellow, you don't think that because I lost that job in the Portobello Road I am at the end of my tether? It happened at a fortunate time, as it were. I am considering several offers. I just can't make up my mind which to accept.

MOSES: [*Grunting*] You better recommend me for one.

HARRIS: Any time, any time... Look old chap, will you do me a favour?

MOSES: I was waiting for that!

HARRIS: It's nothing much... a bit embarrassing, actually. You see, I've no proper place to invite my friends. A spot of bad luck has me in Ladbroke Grove at the moment. A most undesirable area, from which I hope to make a speedy departure. In the meantime, of course, my social activities are somewhat curtailed, if you see what I mean. One can't very well take one's friends to a boarding house in the Grove.

MOSES: Of course not. But then, there's always the Savoy, or the Waldorf?

HARRIS: A nice little room like this would just suit my purpose. If I could have the use of it occasionally?

MOSES: On a sort of commission basis? Like ten shillings an hour?

HARRIS: [*Uneasy laugh*] You must make your little jokes, mustn't you?

MOSES: I'm going to see Bob's fiancee. You better come with me and use some of them high phrases to give she a good impression. I can't talk like you.

HARRIS: Delighted to be of assist, old chap. Though I shan't be able to stay long... I've got to meet an impresario in the West End, but I can always give you a few minutes... About the room, the sort of friends I bring here would actually lend some tone to the place...

Later, Moses and Harris enter the pub and spot Bob and Maureen at a corner table...

MOSES: There's Bob in that corner.

BOB: [*Spotting them and calling*] Moses! Over here! [*They come over*] I thought you weren't coming again!

MOSES: Old Harris here delayed me.

BOB: This is Maureen...

MOSES: Hello...

MAUREEN: Bob talks about you all the time, Moses.

MOSES: This is my friend, Harris...

HARRIS: A pleasure, I'm sure...

BOB: Sit down, sit down... What're you having?

MOSES: Half of bitter for me, Bob.

BOB: Harris?

HARRIS: A gin.

BOB: [*To Maureen*] I'll get you another, Maureen... Shan't be a tick...
[*He goes off for the drinks*]

MAUREEN: How do you like the room?

MOSES: You wouldn't ask if you'd seen the old basement I was living in!

MAUREEN: When're you going back to Trinidad? Aren't you lucky to be getting away from this awful weather!

MOSES: Some time soon... I hope.

HARRIS: Poor Moses has had a most unfortunate time. His plans for returning are always going awry... Isn't that so?

MOSES: [*Meaningfully*] Yes, that's because of the friends I keep... but nothing's going to stand in my way this time. I'll make sure of that...

BOB: [*Returning*] Here we are... [*Sets the drinks on the table and sits*] Well, what do you think of her, Moses? She'll do?

MAUREEN: [*Embarrassed*] Bob! You don't ask things like that!

BOB: Awe, Moses doesn't mind... I like her hair, most. Reminds me of a clump of wild grass!

MAUREEN: Oh, you!

HARRIS: It's lovely hair, actually. It has a lustre and a sheen not often seen in the young women of today.

MAUREEN: There! Thank you, Harris.

MOSES: I agree with Harris, but at the same time, I got to warn you about him. Bob will tell you that he lives in a remote world what ordinary people like us don't know about...

HARRIS: Tut tut! Don't decry my hopes and aspirations, Moses! He is always out for a laugh, Maureen.

BOB: What're you up to these days then, Harris? Met any lords lately?

HARRIS: Actually, I have to be on my way in a few minutes. I am working on a theatre production involving our immigrant population.

MOSES: Save a part for me.

HARRIS: Moses would persist in making fun. I don't think I've got a letter on me at the moment... let's see.. [*He takes out his wallet, and a card falls out on the table*].

MOSES: Look, a flyer drop from your wallet!

MAUREEN: It look like some sort of card.

BOB: Yes... your unemployment card, to draw the dole!

HARRIS: I'll have that! ... I don't seem to have the letter... I must have left it in my evening suit...

MOSES: The thing with the boys, you must of noticed, is how they always good for a laugh, no matter how hard things is!... I was in a good mood when I left the pub... Maureen look all right to me, but then you can't tell from just meeting a person once. She had Bob make me promise to come and see them up in Hampstead after they get married, and I promise that I would, if I was still around... and then, when I get near my room, I notice a van was pull up in front of the house... and a fellar like Galahad standing on the pavement.

GALAHAD: [*As Moses comes up*] Moses! I been waiting here a long time for you.

MOSES: What happen?

GALAHAD: I ain't able to sell that armchair, boy. I try Cap, I try Tolroy... and I even talk to Big City, telling him he could sell it somewhere in the country on one of his long distance trips. But I ain't had any luck.

MOSES: Well that's your business, ain't it? I don't want it. You already give me two pound ten for it.

GALAHAD: I know! The thing is I ain't got no place to keep it. The storeroom shut, and Mr. Joseph got the key. And I can't keep it in the van... I got a small removal job to do.

MOSES: So what you expect me to do?

GALAHAD: Keep it for me a while, Moses, and when I finish the removal, I come back and take it.

MOSES: No sir! That armchair is your property now, and I want nothing to do with it.

GALAHAD: Live and let live, man! I stand to make a good fiver with this job!

MOSES: That's your hard luck, Galahad. Leave it in the park, or on the pavement, but it ain't coming back in my room!

GALAHAD: Not even if I make it worth your while?

MOSES: What you mean?

GALAHAD: Well you sell it for two pound ten, right? I make a deal with you. I sell it back to you!

MOSES: [*Laughing*] You can't catch me, Galahad!

GALAHAD: Let me finish, man! I sell it back to you for ten bob! Ten bob, Moses! That chair have a lot of memories for you. And you still would have that two pounds in your pocket, that I, Galahad, give you!

MOSES: [*Hesitant*] Ten bob?

GALAHAD: Yes! You always feel that I up to some trick, but this time I am the loser! You got my two pounds in your pocket, and you got your chair back... You don't see?

MOSES: Yes... but ten bob...

GALAHAD: Lord, but you hard! That ten bob wouldn't even be mine... I got to buy gasoline for the van.

MOSES: Let me think a little... I just had some drinks...

GALAHAD: It simple as ABC, man! You got a chance now to have one over on me... I can't help it, I got to take the rough with the smooth.

MOSES: It sound all right, but...

GALAHAD: Don't waste time, man! [*He opens the van door*] I late already as it is! Give me a hand to take it inside...

REPORTER: It seems to me that Galahad was still on top of you, Moses. He stood to make a fiver with the removal job, so he could easily have afforded to let the armchair go.

MOSES: It was only afterwards as I was reclining in it, that I realise that. What I should of done was to have made him come back for the chair, and charge him ten shillings for keeping it whilst he was doing the removal job... Still, in the long run, that chair help to take me to Trinidad....

PART SIX: TANTY HAS A HOUSING PROBLEM

REPORTER: Moses, I expect that with your new room, and the job that Bob got for you, you were tempted to forget all about returning to Trinidad?

MOSES: I ain't ever forget that! Although it *was* a temptation. I mean, for the first time in Brit'n I find myself living in a decent room, and this job Bob get for me at the Town Hall wasn't too bad. But you know what was on my mind?

REPORTER: No, tell me.

MOSES: Well, I had this feeling that I could leave whenever I like, that I didn't have to hustle or get into any panic! Before this stage, the situation was frantic to get back home. But now, I wanted to leave in cool blood, to take my time and depart without the feeling as if something was driving me out of the country. You know what I mean?

REPORTER: Yes, but the people who pretended to be your friends...

MOSES: Ah! That's just it! I steer clear of the boys for a long time. I play as if I ain't at home when they come knocking in the Water, and if I see any of them in the streets, I make a tack and dodge in some doorway, or down some side street. Once I seen Galahad in a second-hand car, and he offer me a lift, but he was the last one I wanted to see. In fact, though I keep out of his way, Fate had it in store that I was to hear about him, even if we didn't meet up in person! What happen was this... You remember how he was working for this Mr. Joseph...

In Mr. Joseph's Office in the Portobello Road, Joseph and Galahad are talking...

MR. JOSEPH: Six quid! Is that all you got for that put-u-up? Come, Galahad, you could do better than that.

GALAHAD: It was second-hand, Mr. Joseph. It hard to sell anything to West Indians when it use already. They like to see things bright and shining, with the packing paper still on it.

MR. JOSEPH: Don't hand me that! All the stuff they buy is second-hand. And that put-u-up could sleep four or five in a jam, even if they sleep sideways. You looked for a client with a small room?

GALAHAD: The fellar who buy it living in a room so small he keep talking to his shadow.

MR. JOSEPH: Very funny. Come on. How much you got for it?

GALAHAD: I tell you, Mr. Joseph. Things as a whole ain't going so good for my people. They getting laid off their jobs, they getting less overtime, they have more expenses all round. I was lucky to get six quid off that Barbadian... These Bajans is the tightest immigrants when it comes to money.

MR. JOSEPH: I had a man from Barbados in the shop yesterday and I actually had to stop him buying, so he could have his bus fare home. Come on! I haven't got all day to spend with you.

GALAHAD: You didn't give me a chance to finish... that six quid is only a deposit.

MR. JOSEPH: That's better.

GALAHAD: But we got to pray for the rest. Honestly Mr. Joseph. It look like this Barbadian catching real hell. He ain't got no regular job, he got a wife and family to support...

MR. JOSEPH: I don't employ you to come to me with heartbreak stories. Save all that for our clients. You're pretty good at it, too, except when you try it out on me. I sometimes wonder if I didn't make a mistake taking you on. You haven't come up with any big ideas... but I got something that's right up your alley.

GALAHAD: It's all the expenses I got, you see. If you could manage to let me have a fiver more, I would be able to spread. I can't manage on what I get. Without L S D nobody listens to me.

MR. JOSEPH: If you don't make them listen, I'll get another man.

GALAHAD: I only want to make my position clear.

MR. JOSEPH: I'll make mine clear too. If you muck up this next job, you've had it. You know the Harrow Road? Lots of West Indians live there.

GALAHAD: Like the back of my hand.

MR. JOSEPH: There's a property there I'm interested in. I've got all the tenants out, except a Jamaican family, who are being stubborn...

I've got a name somewhere on my desk... [*Looks*] Yes... you know a chap called Tolroy?

GALAHAD: Tolroy! We used to work together! As a matter of fact his family and me come to this country on the same train.

MR. JOSEPH: Well the problem is that they don't want to move. And I want them to move. You got the general idea?

GALAHAD: Move where? It have children there, and two old women.

MR. JOSEPH: I'm not interested in the family history. I want that house completely vacant by the ending of the week. You understand?

GALAHAD: Sure I understand. But that's a big job, Mr. Joseph.

MR. JOSEPH: You can't handle it?

GALAHAD: What I mean to say is...

MR. JOSEPH: I notice something with you, Galahad. You come in here and try your sales talk. Me! I got you fixed with a car, I put you onto little jobs where you could make something on the side...

GALAHAD: I wouldn't cheat you!

MR. JOSEPH: Don't deny it! I've let you get by with your little drips and drabbles... But this is a big job. I stand to make five hundred quid on the sale of the place, once it's vacant. I don't care how you do it or what you tell them... [*Pause as Galahad hesitates*]... Maybe you'd better stick to second-hand furniture?

GALAHAD: I can handle it.

MR. JOSEPH: Good. Get busy today. This is your chance to get into the big times, boy. Isn't that what you want?

GALAHAD: You going to give me an increase?

MR. JOSEPH: This is a commission job. If you get them out, and the sooner the better for you, we talk about it.

GALAHAD: But how much I could go up to?

MR. JOSEPH: What d'you mean?

GALAHAD: If I got to grease Tolroy or Tanty hand... pass them a little persuasion by way of a few quid?

MR. JOSEPH: Don't make me laugh. If you got to do that, it will be deducted from your commission. And another thing. I don't want no trouble. No business about the Rent Tribunal, or the Citizen's Advice Bureau or anything of the sort. That's why I'm putting you on the job, and by God, if you muck it up, I'll have you wishing you were on the quickest banana boat to Jamaica. Or wherever you come from.

GALAHAD: Leave it to me, Mr. Joseph. Already I got a plan in mind.

MR. JOSEPH: That's ticking, boy. I might consider putting you on a permanent basis. There's a lot we could do for these immigrants, if you're the right man. You've got a chance to prove yourself. I don't want to hear all the talk you've got... Give it to them!...

At Tolroy's House. Tanty is trying to persuade Tolroy to have breakfast...

TANTY: But Tolroy, you can't leave for work with nothing in your stomach!

TOLROY: I tell you I late, Tanty! If I not there, I keep the whole bus.

TANTY: At least have some of this black pudding what Ma buy. I fry it already.

TOLROY: I tell Ma to wake me before she go to work.

TANTY: She forget! She had was to take the children to school on the way... Look the pudding ready. Here... [*She puts it on the table*].

TOLROY: Oh, all right, all right... You ain't have no bread?

TANTY: [*Getting bread*] Here... [*He starts to eat*] You know why you late every day? Is all that staying out at night. That's the trouble. White girls! Nothing else but white girls!

TOLROY: [*With his mouth full*] Leave me alone, Tanty. The way you keep on, you make a man feel as if he still living in Jamaica.

TANTY: The way things looking, we ain't going to have a place to live! I tell you how everybody move out of the house?

TOLROY: Look... if this man come again, the one who say that too many of us living in these two rooms, just keep quiet, eh?

TANTY: Don't say nothing at all? Not even 'morning'?

TOLROY: Tell him to... [*Chokes on his food*] ... just tell him we ain't interested in moving, right?

TANTY: [*Parrot-like*] Yes, tell him we not interested in moving... and then he going to say that all the other tenants move, and why we still here? I done tell him already to come when you home, because I can't talk properly to these people.

TOLROY: I glad you know that, though the rate you carry on make me wonder... Just say you not responsible, and that your nephew Tolroy is the one who pay the rent. You think I could trust you to say that?

102

TANTY: You forget you talking to your elders! You think I can't convey a small message?

TOLROY: You already make me take out insurance that I don't want, and you turn away people I say to call here to see me...

TANTY: Only the white girls, Tolroy! I don't know why you don't look for one of our own girls, it have plenty in the country now.

TOLROY: All right, all right, don't start off again! Hand me my cap off the mantelpiece...

TANTY: [*Getting cap*] If any white person ring the bell, I wouldn't answer. That satisfy you?

TOLROY: I suppose if the postman ring you wouldn't answer?

TANTY: I mean, excepting him, and the coalman, and the gasman... and now and then it have somebody come to full up forms, or ask questions... You want me to shut the door to all these English gentlemen?

TOLROY: [*Savagely*] Just give me the cap... and put less coal on that fire. You and Ma double my coal bill since you come.

TANTY: You don't expect me to stay in this cold room? I not 'custom to the winter yet.

TOLROY: [*Moving to the door, wearily*] All right, Tanty. But do me a favour. Is not too much to ask.

TANTY: What pray?

TOLROY: [*Angrily departing*] Don't answer the bloody door at all! Milkman, insurance man... anybody at all! You understand? We is the only tenants left, so it couldn't be for anybody else!

TANTY: You think I ain't got friends? You think I ain't made friends all this time I been in Londontown? Suppose somebody come to see me... travel all the way from Camden Town, for instance.

TOLROY: [*Exasperated*] Just keep trouble away from the door... You will give me grey hairs before my time...

He goes, slamming the door. Tanty starts clearing up in the room. She starts to talk to herself...

TANTY: ...getting him grey! I age so much since I come to Brit'n... and to hear Tolroy talk like that! I could imagine what it going to be like when the children grow up here. Already I don't understand this funny English they learning at school... and the way they do sums... I never learn like that in Jamaica! ... All well and good for Ma to go to work but who have the most to do?

Slaving here, washing the clothes, keeping the place clean, cooking lunch for the children when they come from school... I tell you! [*The doorbell rings, but she doesn't hear it.*] Me, in my old age, who come hoping to find some peace for my weary bones, and I find I got to work harder in all this snow and... [*The doorbell rings again, more insistently, and Tanty hears it this time*] ... Lord! The doorbell! I best hads peep from the window and see who it is before I go to the door, before Tolroy kill me!

As she peeps, Galahad sees her from the doorstep...

GALAHAD: [*Loudly*] Come on, Tanty! Open the door!

TANTY: Who that there? I don't recognise you properly!

GALAHAD: It's me, Galahad.

TANTY: Oh, Galahad! [*To herself*] Something funny about this fellar that I don't rightly recall... [*Loudly*] What you want? Tolroy says I mustn't open the door!

GALAHAD: I represent the landlord. Open up at once!

TANTY: [*To herself*] Oh lord, the landlord! Still, he's a countryman, he can't mean no evil...

She opens the door and Galahad comes in...

GALAHAD: Tanty! You keeping me out in the cold?

TANTY: I didn't recognise you, Galahad... What you want?

GALAHAD: Don't tell me I come all this way, and Tolroy ain't home!

TANTY: He gone to work.

GALAHAD: But I thought he was working late shift.

TANTY: That was last week.

GALAHAD: I must of got the date wrong, then I got important business, Tanty, important.

TANTY: Come warm yourself by the fire... Tolroy say I burn too much coal. Is all right for him in a warm bus.

GALAHAD: Thanks... Like you got a furnace here... You like it hot, eh?

TANTY: I not as young as I used to be.

GALAHAD: Nothing I can't discuss with you, Tanty, that I couldn't tell Tolroy face to face. You're head of the family, ain't you?

TANTY: Well me son, we not back in Jamaica. I don't know head nor tail in this country, the way how Tolroy treat me. He say I mustn't open the door at all.

GALAHAD: Quite right too. You never know who may step across them thresholds, ready to give you trouble. We have a hard time in this country, Tanty, a hard time... Where the children? Where Ma?

TANTY: Ma working at Lyons, and the children-them at school... But what you wanted to see Tolroy about? Maybe I can help you.

GALAHAD: Maybe you can, maybe you can... How about a cup of tea to help keep out the cold?

TANTY: Yes... I keep the kettle near the fire... [*Moves to it*] What you mean what you said, about the landlord? You not the man does collect the rent!

GALAHAD: No. But I got better connections. Tolroy must of been wondering why all the other tenants left, not so?

TANTY: Oh! You know about that?

GALAHAD: Of course. It's my line of business.

TANTY: Well, is a big mystery to me. The house silent like a grave, and I got to talk to myself for company. What happening, Galahad?

GALAHAD: There's a big redevelopment scheme. All the houses in this street are breaking down... I thought you knew, Tanty. The Council has a plan to erect new buildings... and you got to move. You got to move for sure.

TANTY: [*Awed*] The Council! You mean the Government people?

GALAHAD: No less.

TANTY: Lord! Let me make the tea quick so I could sit down, for the shock! [*She hustles about making the tea*] I know you want plenty sugar... Here Galahad... [*She sits down and sighs*] But tell me something, they can't do that in this country?

GALAHAD: Can't do what, Tanty?

TANTY: Can't put you out on the street? What going to happen to the children? This is white people country, don't forget, Galahad. They have good manners, they have pity and compassion.

GALAHAD: Yes. But the thing is, all of you living in these two rooms. It ain't healthy, and it ain't sanitary. Besides that, the whole house need renovating. Look at that wallpaper, how it peeling off the wall... and listen... [*He gets up and demonstrates*] to these floor boards squeak when I walk on them.

TANTY: But if you know the landlord, you could get him to fix all these things for us?

GALAHAD: It too late for that now. You all got to move before the ending of the week. I giving you formal notice for the landlord, whom I represent. Is a shame Tolroy not here, and I got to give you the news. But you is the head of the family, anyway.

TANTY: Look at my crosses here today! Is how you know all this?

GALAHAD: It's my job. I work for these people.

TANTY: What people. The Council?

GALAHAD: I told you. The owner of the house.

TANTY: You sure you not trying to frighten me? Ain't you the fellar who always up to tricks?

GALAHAD: This is no trick, Tanty. As a matter of fact is only because I know Tolroy personally that I doing my best to warn you before anything happen suddenly. If you don't believe your own people, who you going to believe? That's why I been sent here by the Estate Corporation and Company Limited, because when I hear about it, I decide to come instead of some stranger.

TANTY: Well this is a strange business... Where we going to move to? Places so hard to get, especially with the children.

GALAHAD: That's the problem. But you didn't think I was so cold-hearted to come here with only bad news? From the minute I learn what's happening, I been around my contacts. I might be able to fix you up with a place, a better one, in fact. But I got to warn you we haven't got much time!

TANTY: You know what's the best thing to do? Come back tonight, when Tolroy home. Then you could tell him everything.

GALAHAD: Even tonight going to be too late for this other place. The only way to secure it is to put down a deposit immediately... and also, you got to pay some key money... So if you want me to help, let me know now.

TANTY: I got a few shillings in my purse?

GALAHAD: I mean real money, what you got hid. You have to put down about ten pounds, and say, another ten for the key. I was trying to shift the owner from that sum, but he wouldn't budge any lower.

TANTY: I ain't got such a sum, Galahad... and I suspicion you as soon as you start to talk money.

GALAHAD: [*Getting up*] All right. I'll go. I done my best for you and Ma and the children, because I know Tolroy always saying he wish the lot of you would dead and leave him in peace. I will leave you to sort out your own business.

TANTY: Wait! Which part this place is where we going to move?

GALAHAD: Am... er... not far from here... The children could go to the same school, and you don't have to change your shop or bus route... In fact, if I remember rightly, is the street behind this one.

TANTY: I want to see it before I hand over any money.

GALAHAD: Ah, so you got the money?

TANTY: I ain't say so... but I got to see before we discuss business. Just let me get my coat.

GALAHAD: [*Quickly*] You can't see it now, because the people out to work. But I could contact the owner and pay him so he couldn't let it to anybody else. And if I don't do that today, you lose the chance.

TANTY: Maybe we could find another place?

GALAHAD: Don't make me laugh, Tanty! You know how much trouble that mean? You spend weeks reading all the notice boards, and walking from house to house with the same result, sorry, we full up, or sorry, we don't take coloureds, or sorry, we let the rooms already... You was lucky Tolroy had this place when you land in London, I could tell you.

TANTY: But I ain't got no twenty pounds, Galahad!

GALAHAD: See how much you have in the bedroom. Go on, I wouldn't look. I turning my back...

Tanty goes into the other room...

GALAHAD: [*Louder*] If it wasn't for me, you-all would of had no place to sleep... You could imagine a thing like that in this cold?

TANTY: [*Returning*] I hope I doing the right thing... Here... you count and see how much that is.

GALAHAD: [*Counting*] H'mm... only eight pounds ten shillings, exact.

TANTY: That's all there is, Galahad. Maybe you could go to the owner, being as you know him so well.

GALAHAD: I could try... How soon could you get the balance?

TANTY: When Tolroy come home.

GALAHAD: I'm sorry, Tanty. That's too late. It got to be some time today.

TANTY: Well give me back that money, then.

GALAHAD: I'll keep this... I tell you what I do. You get the rest by this afternoon some time. There must be somebody could lend you the balance. I going to come back about five o'clock.

TANTY: I could see the place then?

GALAHAD: That might be a bit early... but I'll see if I could get a key... Yes, that shouldn't be hard, to get a key... I mean, *the* key... That should prove my good intentions...

Later, at Moses's house. Moses is surprised to find Tanty at his door...

MOSES: [*Alarmed at Tanty's distraught appearance*] What you doing here, Tanty? Somebody dead?

TANTY: Moses! I see so much trouble to find this place, but I too glad I catch you home,

MOSES: You better come in and let me shut the door... [*She enters and Moses shuts the door after her*] ... What happen?

TANTY: We in a big mess... I could sit down?

MOSES: Yes... but I getting ready to go to work...

TANTY: [*Sitting*] I don't know who to turn to in my distress. I spend hours thinking and thinking, and at last your face come to my mind.

MOSES: What... what wrong?

TANTY: It look as if they going put us out on the streets, Moses.

MOSES: I got a lot of worries of my own, Tanty... Who send you here? Tolroy?

TANTY: No, Tolroy ain't home, he don't know the confusion that we in. That's why I come to you. I got nobody to talk with even.

MOSES: Nothing I can do to help... You best wait until Tolroy come home. I mean is none of my business... I late for work, Tanty.

TANTY: I won't keep you back, my son... Is just a little money I want for borrow, till this evening please God. The very minute Tolroy come home, I will get it back from him and bring it myself to give you.

MOSES: You mean to buy rations, or something?

TANTY: No, not that.

MOSES: But what make you feel I have any?

TANTY: You move up here in this grand room, Moses! Is only twelve

108

pounds. I got to get it today to pay for another place. Galahad going come back five o'clock for it.

MOSES: [*Startled*] Galahad! Is *Galahad* you say? What business you got with him?

TANTY: He working for the people what own the house, and he getting another place for me. He trying to help out, you see.

MOSES: Galahad don't help anybody but himself! Listen, Tanty, don't have nothing to do with that man! Anything at all! The amount of time he swindle me.

TANTY: You don't understand, Moses. Is just you one here, but we is a whole family in the Harrow Road. Galahad say...

MOSES: I don't want to hear nothing what he say! I warning you, you best hads wait till Tolroy come home.

TANTY: It going to be too late. The man might let the rooms to someone else!

MOSES: [*Laughing to himself*] To tell you the truth, if it was anybody else, I might have listened to you, which is the most I can do. But you have no idea what you putting yourself in for.

TANTY: [*Beginning to cry*] Look Moses, just imagine as if me, Tanty, come to ask you to lend me twelve pounds. What would you say?

MOSES: I keep saying it, Tanty, but you not listening! I would say I wish I could help you, if I had it.

TANTY: I know you got money, Moses. You not no spendthrift nor vagabond like those other fellars... Is none of them I could turn to in my distress.

MOSES: I want to have nothing to do with Galahad, directly or indirectly. You playing with fire, I tell you!

TANTY: [*Choked voice*] I don't know what going to happen now... Those poor children out in the cold, no place to sleep...

MOSES: You have my sympathy... but I know that man too well.

TANTY: [*Sniffing*] That's why I say, that is me you lending the money to. Not him. And not even Tolroy... First time such a catastrophe happen to me in my old age, in this country, and I thought you would help me, Moses, you is the only one who...

MOSES: I got to go to work, Tanty. You must be patiente until Tolroy come home. He will fix everything. He knows all about landlords and rents and looking for rooms.

TANTY: [*Sobbing now*] We all got crosses to bear... but I never thought at this time of my life you would treat somebody who like your own mother... [*She bursts out crying. Moses is silent for a few seconds. Then...*]

MOSES: [*Angrily*] All right, all right! Here! [*He moves to the mantelpiece, picks up his wallet and takes out money*] Five... ten... eleven... twelve. Remember what you say. I lending you, *Tanty,* this money. Not Tolroy, or Ma or anybody else. And you *sure* you bringing it back for me this evening?

TANTY: [*Effusive relief*] Look, I kiss the cross, Moses! [*She makes a cross with her fingers and kisses it loudly*] Just the moment he appear on the doorstep! God bless you, my son! It still have some good people in the world!

MOSES: I never lucky enough to meet, them, though.

TANTY: I best hads get back quick, eh, before Galahad come...

MOSES: Don't call that man name! I don't want to know what business you got with him; it's your own funeral.

TANTY: You take a big weight off my back, Moses! God will bless you...

MOSES: All I want is my money back this evening... And you better go quick before I change my mind, Tanty...

[*Narrating voice*] That was always the trouble with me, soft heart... but I don't like to see old people suffer... You got to trust somebody, else you lose all the things you believe in... I was sure Galahad was up to something, but she wouldn't listen to me... That evening I come home early and sit down in my room waiting, and to tell you the truth, as the minutes tick by and I ain't seeing Tanty, I begin to get that old familiar feeling that I know so well... That once again, after all my experiences and resolutions, I was the one who would be left holding the sticky end of the stick... I was wishing that Bob was here to console me, when I hear a knock at the door...

Bob comes into the room, to be greeted warmly by Moses...

MOSES: Bob! I was just thinking of you, boy. Come in.

BOB: I figure you must of lost my Hampstead address, so I came to remind you of it.

MOSES: Such a lot on my mind, Bob. I'll come one of these days, honestly... How Maureen keeping?

BOB: Fine, fine... As a matter of fact, we might be having a family soon.

110

MOSES: Well! Look at that, eh! A new generation. You don't waste time!

BOB: Not like you... When're you leaving for home?

MOSES: Not too long again, Bob... just a few things to sort out...

BOB: Umm... [*Slight pause*] How's the job, then? How're you getting on with old Charlie at the Town Hall.

MOSES: If *you* didn't get that job for me, Bob, I would of left it! He keeps finding fault with everything I do.

BOB: Charlie's like that with everybody, not to worry... You fixed up with the landlord about renewing the lease for the room?

MOSES: I don't know about that, Bob... it costing me a lot to live here.

BOB: You don't want to go back down to that basement downstairs, do you?

MOSES: At least people know I didn't have money when I was there. But up here, they feel I must be a millionaire or something. Tanty was here today begging.

BOB: Don't tell me you got into a mess again!

MOSES: She coming back with the money, though... I thought it was she at the door when you came.

BOB: How much?

MOSES: Eh? What?

BOB: Come on, how much she stuck you for?

MOSES: Twelve quid.

BOB: Oh, hell. I don't understand you, Moses. After all you've been through with these people!

MOSES: They was going to put them out on the streets, Bob! She had to try and get another place!

BOB: That's a lot of nonsense to start with! People don't get put out like that. There are new laws about a tenancy, don't you know?

MOSES: Well anyway, Tanty not like them other fellars, she don't try no fast one.

BOB: Trouble with you is you don't know about these things. No landlord could put anybody out on the streets. And why you had to get yourself involved in Tolroy and Tanty's business is beyond me. I always told you...

A knock at the door interrupts him...

111

MOSES: [*Brightly*] That must be Tanty now. You see? It wasn't nothing to worry about... [*He opens the door. Cap is there.*]

CAP: Ah bo! I glad I meet you home, oh.

MOSES: [*Groaning*] It's you, Cap... I thought it was Tanty.

CAP: [*With a snigger*] You must be really rusty, boy! Hello, Bobbo.

BOB: What you selling tonight, Cap?

MOSES: Yes. What breeze blow you round here? [*He shuts the door*].

CAP: I plead not guilty. I here on innocent business for the party.

BOB: What party?

CAP: The one for OUR PEOPLE, Bob. The time has come when we got to organise and look after our rights, else we all get left in the lurch.

BOB: You chaps are always forming some group or committee, and they just come and go.

MOSES: That's right. We still in the same predicament, standing in the same spot.

CAP: You think so? Then you must come to the protest march on Sunday. We start at Hyde Park Corner, and we collect in Trafalgar Square, then on to Downing Street to see the Prime Minister.

MOSES: What protest?

CAP: You don't have to have anything special to protest about... as long as you against the Government and the country. I got placards at home, you can have one... you too, Bob. We not a racial party.

BOB: You got a hope, Cap, if you find me marching with you.

MOSES: And for my part, Sunday morning is the only time I have to sleep late.

CAP: Ah, that's the trouble, I can't get recruits... but sooner or later you will have to join the ranks, Moses, You could still help out, though, with my survey.

BOB: Now he's doing a survey! What about?

CAP: I making notes of cases where our people suffer unnecessary hardships, and come face to face with prejudice and so on.

BOB: Then what? You type them out and take them to Downing Street?

CAP: All well and good for you, Bob. You could afford to laugh...

BOB: I'm not laughing! But for heaven's sake, I don't see what good a bloke like you could do.

CAP: Never mind Bob, Moses. Look I got my notebook here... Now, you remember anything what happen to you, like when you went to look for a job, or a place to live?

MOSES: Man Cap, put away that notebook and behave yourself. What experiences I had, I saving for when I write my book about life in the Mother Country.

CAP: Ah bo! That sound interesting. I must tell the committee about it. Let me make a note... We could find you a publisher...

BOB: You're just wasting time, Moses. Better to get around to Harrow Road and see what's keeping Tanty. I'll come with you if you like.

MOSES: You right, Bob.

CAP: Maybe I can get a story from that Jamaican family.

MOSES: As a matter of fact, right now they in some confusion about having to move.

CAP: Oh? Good! Some ruthless landlord throwing them out on the streets? I should of brought my camera and take some pictures.

BOB: Let's get a move on and stop hanging around...

At Harrow Road; Tolroy and Tanty are having a big quarrel.

TOLROY: Lord, Lord! What you put me in here tonight? More calamity?

TANTY: You call it calamity when I take it upon my good self to go to all that trouble to make sure we got a roof over our heads? I was in tears begging Moses for that money!

TOLROY: Before I went out this morning I warn you... and which part you think I going to get twelve pounds to pay Moses?

TANTY: I promise him, Tolroy! I got to give him back tonight!

TOLROY: And this man Galahad! How you know he was really working for the landlord? I wash my hands of the whole business. If you think…

A knock at the door interrupts him...

TOLROY: Go and see who that is... in fact, I better go myself.

He opens the door on Moses, Cap and Bob

CAP: Hello, bo.

113

MOSES: I was expecting Tanty, Tolroy. What happen?

TOLROY: Come in, come... she right here ... [*They enter room*] I telling you in front, Moses, that I don't know nothing about no arrangement you make with this woman. I just barely come home from work – I ain't even eat food yet – and she telling me some rigmarole story about Galahad and borrowing money from you...

TANTY: Don't listen to him, Moses. When he cool off I will get your money for you, before you go.

CAP: I am doing a survey on discrimination, Tolroy. You tell me the whole story and I will write it down in this notebook and present the case to the committee.

TOLROY: I don't know nothing! I come home, and this woman say she give Galahad twenty pounds for some new place to live. That's all I know.

MOSES: If I can get a word in, Tolroy, all I interested in is my money. If you give me, I will depart and leave you in peace.

TOLROY: What money? *I* didn't borrow anything from you, Moses!

MOSES: Well then, you, Tanty. My twelve pounds, if you please.

TANTY: Don't let me down here tonight, Tolroy!

TOLROY: You won't get it from *me,* I tell you! You go and hustle a job somewhere washing dishes, and pay back Moses!

CAP: About the survey... Who is the landlord? Some brutal white man, eh? And this place look so dilapidated. Let me take some notes...

BOB: [*Loudly*] Look, I know it's none of my business, but honestly you lot act as if you are completely stupid! Don't you know that there are laws to protect you against people like Galahad? You're not going to let him get away with this, are you?

TANTY: You right, Mr. Bob! Look I got some evidence. When Galahad come back this evening, I get this from him... [*She takes out a key and plonks it on the table*].

TOLROY: What's that?

TANTY: You can't see it's a key? To the new house we going live in.

BOB: All right. So he left a key. Where's the place?

TANTY: In the next street. Number 36A.

BOB: You've been to see it?

TANTY: I was waiting for Tolroy. But he ain't give me a chance to explain nothing.

TOLROY: [*Taking key*] I going and see this place, right now.

BOB: That's the most sensible thing that's been said so far.

TOLROY: Moses, you and Bob come with me, so I would have witnesses.

CAP: I will stay and chat with Tanty, bo. I want all the information. It sound to me like a classic case of racial discrimination, with some underhanded business on the side. Tell me, Tanty, do you get prompt service in the shops, or you find you always last in the queue to get attention...

Moses, Tolroy and Bob are walking down the street

MOSES: I get a funny feeling tonight, Bob.

BOB: Let's see what happens... What's the number on the gate, Tolroy?

TOLROY: Thirty-two.

BOB: Just a couple more houses... Here. This must be thirty-six.

MOSES: Yes. But what we want is thirty-six A.

TOLROY: Maybe it on the other side of the street.

BOB: Don't fool yourself.

MOSES: Over there is only odd numbers. And this is the last house in the street. I could of told you the outcome of this little stroll without taking the trouble to come. Mr. Galahad just push his hand in a hat and come up with a number, and it happen to be thirty-six. He just add the 'A' for style.

BOB: My God, I'm beginning to wonder if you people actually enjoy being taken for a ride by Galahad!

TOLROY: But the key, man!

BOB: What's a key? You think they're hard to come by?

TOLROY: Maybe thirty six A is the top part... I better ask.

MOSES: Please yourself...

Tolroy pushes the gate and knocks on the door. An irate owner opens.

OWNER: What d'you want?

TOLROY: Excuse me... I was looking for thirty-six A, please...

OWNER: No number like that on this street. This is thirty-six. We haven't a thirty-six A.

TOLROY: [*As owner is about to shut door*] Wait! Am... just let me try this key in your lock, please... I want to... [*He tries it quickly...*] It don't fit! Sorry mister!

115

BOB: So what are you going to do now? More talk?

TOLROY: [*Full of fury*] I going to make a charge with the police against Galahad. I not going to take no swindle as easy as you, Moses.

MOSES: You can charge him with murder for all I care. I just want my money back tonight. Tanty promise me.

BOB: You must have been mad to give her money, Moses. I can't sympathise with you.

MOSES: Galahad sure to be at that protest march in Trafalgar Square on Sunday, Tolroy.

TOLROY: Good. On top of the court case, I going to that march with a heavy banner, and I will beat him like a snake.

BOB: That would be worth seeing. Let's go and help him, Moses...

PART SEVEN: MOSES BOOKS A PASSAGE

The scene is set in Trafalgar Square at the political rally. There are indistinct cries, the occasional shout, traffic noises and a general hubbub in the background. Moses, Bob, Tolroy and Tanty have come to the meeting in hopes of seeing Galahad. Tolroy is all worked up and ready for a fight with him...

BOB: I don't think you should have taken that flag off that pole, Tolroy. There are police here to control the crowd, and it now looks as if you are armed.

TOLROY: You think I care. You just look for Galahad, and when you see the scamp, woe betide him.

TANTY: Amen. But I want to do something, Tolroy.

TOLROY: [*Growling*] You just get here, man! You can't hold it back a few minutes?... You keeping a sharp eye out, Moses?

MOSES: I don't think Galahad going to turn up myself, though Cap said he was going to contribute some free second-hand furniture for them to sit down on the platform.

TANTY: I keep telling you, Tolroy, I want to do something. Bad!

TOLROY: [*Ignoring Tanty*] What you think, Bob? We should hang around and wait?

BOB: I don't know about you and Moses, but I got to get back home.

MOSES: I told you that would happen as soon as you decide to get married! It didn't take long, Bob.

BOB: It's just a waste of time, isn't it?... unless you think Cap is going to speak.

MOSES: Who want to hear Cap? Those people up there serious, man. All Cap doing, if you observe, is shifting around the chairs and adjusting the microphones... [*There is a technical disturbance on the loud speaker...*] and even that he can't do well, as you just hear!

TANTY: Excuse me, Mr. Bob, but you know where the ladies is?

BOB: Sure… just nip down in the underground… should be one there.

TANTY: Thank you… [*She starts to go*] … Oh, Moses, don't go away, I want to see you. [*She goes quickly*]

MOSES: What Tanty want to see me for, Tolroy?

TOLROY: I don't know, man… Look, I going to scout around on the other side of the square, and see if I see this man. If you all hear a riot going on over there, you will know that I have found him…

BOB: [*Calling out after him*] Don't behave foolishly, Tolroy, there are police around… [*Tolroy leaves*] Oh well, why the hell should I worry? You coming, Moses?

MOSES: Where you going?

BOB: I told you, home, to Hampstead. Maureen is waiting… You could cook us that big West Indian meal at last.

MOSES: I best had wait and see what Tanty want… Anyway, you got to get special things for that cook-up, boy, if you want to taste the real thing. And today is Sunday, all the shops closed.

BOB: When're you coming then?

MOSES: Leave it for one day in the week. I will phone you.

BOB: You sure?

MOSES: Yes… make it Tuesday… I leaving work early.

BOB: Tell me what you need. I'll get the stuff.

MOSES: No fears! You'll just muddle up yourself… Leave it to me.

BOB: Right… I'm going, then. And if I were you, I'd get back home and catch up on some sleep. You got nothing to learn at these marches, Moses. I'm sorry I allowed you to encourage me.

MOSES: I know, I only came because I thought Cap would of talked… I'll just wait to see Tanty, and then straight home.

BOB: [*On his way*] Let me know if Tolroy got a hold of Galahad…

MOSES: [*Shouts to departing Bob*] Galahad must be sleeping the whole morning away, while we hope he would turn up here.

Bob goes. Cap comes up to Moses, all agitated.

CAP: Moses! Who is here!

MOSES: How you mean 'Who is here?' Who you expect, Prince Philip?

CAP: You never know your luck!… but seriously, I mean among the boys?

MOSES: The only one I seen is Tolroy, who looking for Galahad to wash him with licks.

CAP: What happened to Bart? Big City? and Harris? Yes, Harris! He ain't around?

MOSES: Not that I know of, why?

CAP: Well you can't see the trend of the speeches? What is happening is that all the coloured countries have speakers, except the West Indies! And we ain't got much more time... You could speechify?

MOSES: What you want with me? Can't it have one man up there who talking for all the coloured people in Brit'n?

CAP: That's just it, Moses! So far we had a fellar from Ceylon, another from Gambia and another from Kenya. And all of them talking about their own country, as if they want to divert the immigration waves from Mother Brit'n! You ain't been listening?

MOSES: Well we just hanging on the edges here... We didn't come to listen to no rarse speech, we only come to beat Galahad.

CAP: Well I can't talk for the West Indies! I am a Nigerian who will return home to rule twenty tribes...

MOSES: You better get up there and talk for Nigeria.

CAP: It is time for the West Indian, man! Is the boys from the islands who causing all the botheration in London. The committee ask me to get somebody quick...

MOSES: Well here is Tolroy returning from his search... [*Tolroy comes back looking frustrated*] ... Tolroy! Cap want you to make speech.

TOLROY: Forget that speech rarse... You seen Galahad, Cap?

CAP: This is politics now, man! You got a chance to go up there and say a few words... I will give you my notebook, which contains several cases of open discrimination...

TOLROY: You must be mad! You think I would go up there and risk some executive from London Transport seeing me raising rarse in Trafalgar Square? As it is, my job in jeopardy by being here this morning: I hope nobody in the Transport seen me!

CAP: What is this then, Moses? Ain't you got a representative anywhere in the crowd? Where's Harris, man?

MOSES: He ain't here, I told you already!

CAP: Then never let it be said, in the future, that I didn't give you and the boys an opportunity...

TANTY: [*Coming back suddenly*] You all find Galahad? I got a big milk bottle here in my handbag, to bust on his head...

TOLROY: [*Growling*] Just stand back there in the crowd and keep your mouth quiet, woman. This ain't no sufferage meeting.

MOSES: Unless Cap want Tanty to talk on the platform? She's a Jamaican immigrant, she live some years in the country...

CAP: [*Quick interruption*] I rather have Tolroy... Come with me, Tolroy, and see the notes I got. You might change your mind. But we ain't got much time... [*Cap and Tolroy go off.*]

TANTY: What that all about, Moses?

MOSES: Oh, they need somebody to make a speech.

TANTY: Where from? Jamaica?

MOSES: I suppose anywhere in the Caribbean!

TANTY: Oh! Because if they want somebody from Jamaica, I could go, you know.

MOSES: I can't stay, Tanty... What it is you wanted to see me about?

TANTY: The money, Moses! I too shame I wasn't able to give you back!

MOSES: Oh, that. You could forget it. This ain't the first time that sort of thing happen to me.

TANTY: But I worried, Moses! I promise you that money back off my own head! I know how everybody take advantage of your good nature, and I don't want you to feel that I do the same thing.

MOSES: Rest easy, Tanty... I got nothing against you. Was Galahad who fool you.

TANTY: That rogue! You know where I could catch a hold of him?

MOSES: I don't know where he living now, but I know he working for that Mr. Joseph who got a shop in Portobello Road... You know it?

TANTY: Sure I know it! So that's where he is, eh? I will get after him. Before I done, Moses, I will make up everything to you... Watch... [*She makes the sign of the cross with two fingers and kisses it loudly*] ... There! I swear on the cross... I will change your fortune and get you back to Trinidad, don't worry...

MOSES: [*With a small laugh*] You got your own burdens, Tanty... I will take care of my own...

Next morning. Tanty is fully determined to prove to Moses her good intentions... She is having a word with Ma, who is ready to go to work...

120

MA: ... I don't know why you keeping on and on! I told you already. It ain't got no more vacancies.

TANTY: It always have vacancies to wash up and work in the kitchen!

MA: [*Discouraging*] Well even if it have, they don't want nobody as old as you. You think that work easy? Here you wash two-three plates, and a cup and saucer. There, in the tea-shop, you know how much? Is like mountains in front of you sometimes, and hundreds of customers waiting...

TANTY: So just because I have a little rheumatic pain, you feel I can't do that work? Ever since I did come from Jamaica I did make up my mind to work, Ma.

MA: Why you don't rest yourself in peace, Tanty? All you have to do is look after the place and tend the children. It's just the sort of job for you.

TANTY: You can say that. Poor Moses trust me and lend me money, and I haven't got it to pay him back! If you and Tolroy feel I can't do nothing, why the both of you don't make up that money and give me, so I could go to that poor boy and pay him back.

MA: The way you get on, you would think he from home. But Moses is a Trinidadian, you forgetting! Them Trinidadians and Barbadians and Grenadians, or whatever else besides Jamaica, you can't trust them yourself! ... Aha!

TANTY: What?

MA: Is how you don't know this Mr. Moses and this Mr. Galahad plan the whole thing together? We Jamaicans can't trust these Trinidadians, you know! They always feel they smarter than we!

TANTY: You talking 'bout poor Moses that everybody take advantage of? My child, I hear how he trying so hard to get back to Trinidad and everything happening against him.

MA: There! That's what I mean! You see how they smart? Don't forget he been in this country donkeys years! He know which part to get butter when his bread dry, I can tell you. These Trinidadians ain't fall off no tree! That's why the politics don't work!

TANTY: Politics? How that come into it, pray?

MA: Well, you yourself! You can't see what going to happen in the end? Right now, is black man for black man, but later on, it going to be black man for countryman, and Jamaican for Jamaican, and so on!

TANTY: I don't believe you, Ma! Moses been friends with Tolroy for years... and this fellar, Cap, who from Nigeria! The boys don't have no colour problem! You don't come to the meetings in Trafalgar Square, so you don't know what happening! The latest is Black Power against White Power, in case you want to know!

MA: [*Sneering*] Listen, them kinds of things happen in Jamaica... It ain't have nothing like Black Power in this God's world, nor White Power, for that matter! Take for instance, the Spaniards; or for that matter, the Germans-them, who kill all those white people in the war! Is who we fighting?... The English? The English-them given me my bread and butter, child! I can't march against them just because they happen to be white!

TANTY: All the same, whichever way the tide goes, you got to think of your people, and I intend to get that money for Moses, and see that he left Brit'n if he want to.

MA: Well you can't talk about working at all. The onlyest reason I work, is because I know you here home to take care of the place, and look after the children. In fact, if you get a job, Tolroy would put you out right away, I warning you... You should count your blessings instead of looking for more worries...

Later. Tanty is at Joseph's shop in the Portobello Road. She has come to look for Galahad...

MR. JOSEPH: I'm a busy man, Mrs. Whatever-your-name. Is it about a purchase you made some time ago? My guarantee is only good if...

TANTY: You Mr. Joseph?

MR. JOSEPH: Yes, but I told you...

TANTY: I am looking for Gal... Mr. Galahad...

MR. JOSEPH: [*Under his breath*] Oh... shit... He doesn't actually work for me. He does odd jobs, that's all. I haven't the faintest idea where he can be found, I'm sorry...

TANTY: [*Indignant*] What! The man work for you and you don't know where he is?

MR. JOSEPH: You his mother? Or some relative?

TANTY: God forbid! I am Tanty, and I live in the Harrow Road with Tolroy...

MR. JOSEPH: Oh... that... Well, I've given up the whole deal... This is about the place where you live, I take it?

TANTY: Not really. I only interested in learning Mr. Galahad's whereabouts...

MR. JOSEPH: [*Concerned with the property deal*] That's all behind the drain, with me... You can live as long as you like in Harrow Road, Mrs.... er... Tanty. Everything cleared up. You understand? [*He labours this, thinking that all West Indians are gullible*] ... You- got-nothing-to-worry-about... [*Also he wants to get rid of her*]... You stay there... no more move... savvy? Catch?

TANTY: Mr. Joseph! We not as stupid as we appear, you know! I have to put it to you that Mr. Galahad come and get twelve pounds off me, Tanty, for some new place that didn't exist...

MR. JOSEPH: [*Soft chuckle*] Did he now, the little bastard! And he told me to forget the deal completely when he reported.

TANTY: I don't know the ins and outs of your business, Mr. Joseph, but if you will kindly tell me where I could find him, I will be satisfied... That's all I want.

MR. JOSEPH: When I got Galahad here, I thought I would have him under my thumb... [*Laughs again, treats Galahad's gain with fellowship humour*]... The little bastard! Anyway, Mrs. Tanty, it is the company policy not to divulge the addresses of employees, unless we have some fair idea of what's what... you know what I mean... like that twelve pounds?

TANTY: Well I didn't have that great amount of money on me Mr. Joseph? You ought to know better than to treat poor people that way.

MR. JOSEPH: I had nothing to do with it, my dear... Is that chair comfortable? Would you like a cool drink? I observe that you tend to fan yourself with your skirt... entirely unnecessary, I assure you. We got air-conditioning here... You say you gave Galahad twelve pounds.

TANTY: Which I expect back, Mr. Joseph, from you, as his employer. I don't have to look for him no more.

MR. JOSEPH: [*Thinking about Galahad*] That boy! He'll always stay in second-hand furniture... I shouldn't have got him to come to you... I could let you have that twelve pounds in a moment, but I have to know a bit more.

TANTY: I borrow that money from Moses to pay Galahad, you see! And now I got to get it. I in a bad position, Mr. Joseph, and I honest-to-God expect you to help me, seeing as you know how to ease up the difficulties of our people. I thought of going to the Rent Tribunal people...

MR. JOSEPH: You don't want to confuse yourself with the Government, Tanty... if it is only the matter of twelve pounds...

TANTY: Galahad is the one should pay Moses. I don't want for him to get into trouble, you see. That's why I telling you all this.

MR. JOSEPH: Quite. Now, you listen to me, Mrs. Tanty. That twelve pounds is as safe as if you had it in the suitcase under your bed, believe you me... Forget about it.

TANTY: But I have to give it back to Moses! The poor boy been saving up his money for years to go back to Trinidad...

MR. JOSEPH: I can let you have twelve pounds worth of goods from the shop... No, I tell you what. I will let you take anything you like up to twelve pounds and ten shillings.., yes, ten SHILLINGS extra. You don't get a bargain like that every day, Mrs. Tanty!

TANTY: I don't see how that would help poor Moses. What he want is the cash...

MR. JOSEPH: [*He is getting the germ of an idea*] Say! You talking about the chap who's going back home? I know all about that! He brought his tropical outfit here! I thought he was back in the islands by now!

TANTY: Lots of difficulties that boy had to face, Mr. Joseph, you wouldn't believe. Everybody take advantage of him, borrow money and don't pay back, eat his food, use up his time, get him to use his savings.., so that up to now, he ain't get much nearer to this idea of leaving Brit'n.

MR. JOSEPH: [*Thinking of means to exploit these facts*] I see... I see... Look, er... Tanty, will you trust me?

TANTY: No!

MR. JOSEPH: Not even if I told you that I would get that boy back to Jamaica, or wherever, if it's the last thing I do?

TANTY: *You,* Mr. Joseph?

MR. JOSEPH: Well I couldn't do it without your help.

TANTY: I would be satisfy if you give me the twelve pounds I owe Moses.

MR. JOSEPH: And lose a chance to help him on his way? To actually get him on a plane and out of the country?

TANTY: But... but how?

MR. JOSEPH: You leave it all to me. You free to do a job?

TANTY: I made up my mind I would work somehow and get that money back.

MR. JOSEPH: Good, good. You're working for me... in the shop. Eight pounds a week.

TANTY: Eight pounds!.. Doing what, pray?

MR. JOSEPH: Just bringing the customers in. You let it be known that I will put aside... er... a certain percentage, of all the money they spend in the shop, towards Moses's passage. In fact, Tanty... [*The idea is getting hold of him*] we will do more than that... You've got just the face for an advertisement in the local papers...

TANTY: You want my photo too?

MR. JOSEPH: Yes, you will see yourself in a big display...

TANTY: But to come back to this percentage business... How much, in actual money?

MR. JOSEPH: Enough to see him clear of these shores! Isn't that what he wants? You don't have to bother about what it costs... that's the headache of Joseph and Company Incorporated!

TANTY: [*Hesitant*] I best discuss this with my nephew, Tolroy, Mr. Joseph. I always get into trouble when I do something on my own.

MR. JOSEPH: What's there to discuss? Look, I'm going out of my way to help you and Mr. Mosely. Is that all the gratitude you people have? This could be a big thing, Tanty. It might even lead to you getting a permanent job with me.

TANTY: You mean regular work?

MR. JOSEPH: Exactly... The idea is taking hold of me. We could start up a little campaign to bring the customers rolling in... [*He gives a small contented chuckle*] It's great, Tanty, it's great! Here, have a cigar!

TANTY: [*Taken aback*] I... I doesn't smoke, Mr. Joseph.

MR. JOSEPH: Just as well... Now, ready to start?

TANTY: You mean right now?

MR. JOSEPH: No time like the present. That's the success of my business. We get an idea, and move on fast...

TANTY: Well, I have to run home first. I got to make some arrangements with the children-them, you see...

MR. JOSEPH: Okay, have a couple of hours off... and Tanty, when you come back, bring a few with you, eh?

TANTY: A few... what?

MR. JOSEPH: Customers! By that time I'll have a photographer to take your picture...

Later, in Joseph's shop. Galahad has turned up...

MR. JOSEPH: Where the hell have you been, Galahad?

GALAHAD: The van broke down, Mr. Joseph...

MR. JOSEPH: All right. I'll have that twelve quid you got off that job in the Harrow Road.

GALAHAD: What twelve quid is this?

MR. JOSEPH: Come on, Tanty was here!

GALAHAD: I... I ain't got it, Mr. Joseph.

MR. JOSEPH: How much you got left, you little bastard?

GALAHAD: About five... I think.

MR. JOSEPH: Give it here... [*Galahad reluctantly gives it to him*] I'll dock the rest from your pay. With interest.

GALAHAD: [*Pleading*] Live and let live, Mr. Joseph.

MR. JOSEPH: That's *my* motto, boy... Now listen to me... You know this chap Mosely?

GALAHAD: Which Mosely this?

MR. JOSEPH: The one who's going back to Jamaica.

GALAHAD: You mean Moses?

MR. JOSEPH: Yeah, that's the guy.

GALAHAD: He and me is good friends.

MR. JOSEPH: That's fine. I want you to bring him here.

GALAHAD: Bring Moses here? What for?

MR. JOSEPH: Just do as I say.

GALAHAD: [*Foreseeing difficulties*] Am... er, I don't know... we was very friendly one time, but he acts funny with me these days...

MR. JOSEPH: It doesn't look as if I could depend on you for anything, Galahad, except to try and chisel me!

GALAHAD: That's not true... I mean, if you give me an idea what it's about...

MR. JOSEPH: [*With heavy sarcasm*] You think you'll understand? Let's try anyway... I want to do a campaign with the customers, see, promise them cut prices, and a percentage of what they spend in the shop goes to a sort of fund to send Mosely back to Jamaica... You sort of follow?

GALAHAD: That's a great idea, Mr. Joseph!

MR. JOSEPH: Yeah... well, I got Tanty roped in all ready... You got anything to suggest?

GALAHAD: I thinking hard... Let me see... I know the sort of fellar he is; he won't come to the shop.

MR. JOSEPH: Well... You think you can get a photo of him?

GALAHAD: I could try!... I don't know if he got any...

MR. JOSEPH: If I let you have one of those cameras in the shop, which any baby can operate...

GALAHAD: Yes, that might work! And... I thinking hard, Mr. Joseph, as you can see.

MR. JOSEPH: Don't strain yourself.

GALAHAD: I mean, being in the second-hand furniture trade, I notice that he got an old armchair there in his room!

MR. JOSEPH: What the hell has that got to do with it?

GALAHAD: I was just thinking hard... Suppose I get a photo of him sitting down in the chair... and... am, suppose I get the chair too... I got to buy it off him, of course, for a few pounds... and then... seeing as how he spent most of his years in Brit'n sitting in that chair, we could maybe auction it off, like, to the people... being as it would have sentimental value, like...

MR. JOSEPH: Sit down, Galahad, rest yourself. My! That must have hurt!

GALAHAD: You think it would work, Mr. Joseph?

MR. JOSEPH: I'll get somebody working on it.

GALAHAD: It's my idea, man!

MR. JOSEPH: You'll only muck it up.

GALAHAD: No. Give me a chance... I could do it! And the thing is, that we mustn't let Moses know anything... he mightn't like the idea. It's only that old Tanty might open her big mouth...

MR. JOSEPH: I'll take care of Tanty.

GALAHAD: It's a good idea, Mr. Joseph! You could make a lot of money off a deal like this! I know plenty customers would come to the shop and...

MR. JOSEPH: All right. Don't keep on, get moving. Action is what I like...

Later, Moses is in his room, preparing for a disheartening move back to the basement. He is shifting some things around when there is a knock at the door. He opens to see Galahad...

MOSES: Aha! The hunchback of Notre Dame!

GALAHAD: What the joke about?

MOSES: Well I expect you to be shouting, 'Sanctuary! Sanctuary!' because everybody in town out for your head. Including me.

GALAHAD: Ah, don't mind that, man... You moving?

MOSES: Back to the basement. I can't afford to live high like you fellars... I suppose you better come in, though I ain't got nothing to eat. Or drink. Or smoke. [*He shuts the door*]

GALAHAD: Have a cigar, Moses.

MOSES: Anything you got to give, I will take... ta... [*They light up*].

GALAHAD: I come on serious business.

MOSES: I can see that, with the camera you sporting. You selling dirty pictures now?

GALAHAD: Don't lark, man. I come back for that armchair there. Five pounds. Cash. You want it?

MOSES: What's all this interest in my old armchair? Your conscience pricking you for all the money you diddle off me, or what?

GALAHAD: Well... yes... something like that.

MOSES: Five pounds, eh? You think it worth as much as that? The last time you was forcing yourself to give me two pound ten for it,

GALAHAD: I got a customer.

MOSES: No doubt, otherwise what would you do with it? How much the customer giving for it?

GALAHAD: I don't know. I might even get less than the five I pay... but as you say, my conscience pricking me.

MOSES: Well, well! The great Galahad who living a high life in the big times decide to do a good deed! Boy, I wish I could believe you.

GALAHAD: Is true, Moses. If I lie, I die.

MOSES: Ah, you know the old poetry we learn in school, 'Cowards die many times before their deaths.'

GALAHAD: And not only that, but before you leave the shores of Brit'n you will have cause to thank me, Galahad, for the things I do for you.

MOSES: You better don't say anything more, Galahad. You breaking my heart. Let we just talk about the armchair. How much you said? Six pounds?

GALAHAD: Five.

MOSES: Make it six.

GALAHAD: Well...

MOSES: Make it seven.

GALAHAD: Stop making joke, man Moses!

MOSES: Well seven not too much! I had to change the cover last year, and mend the springs... Let me see how conscience-stricken you really is... eight?

GALAHAD: You would never make a businessman; that's why you ain't progress in this country!

MOSES: That's better, you now sounding like your true self.

GALAHAD: Well I can't spend all day. I give you six pounds, and that's as high as I could go. And I got the money right here... Look. [*Takes out the money*] ... A fiver and a pound.

MOSES: Take care it ain't counterfeit money you passing on me!

GALAHAD: [*Laughing*] I ain't reach up to them big times yet!

MOSES: [*Taking the money*] All right. Six pounds, off Galahad the Great, for an old armchair... You know, I would of given it to you for nothing, because I only going back to the basement for a couple of weeks or so, and then, I am out of the country, believe it or not.

GALAHAD: I believe you this time!

MOSES: I don't care if you do or you don't... I finish with all you fellars. Selfish and ungrateful, the whole lot of you.

GALAHAD: Let bygones be bygones, man... Look, I ain't even have a photo of you, to remind me what you look like when you gone! Let's take a picture.

MOSES: You want to look at it and remember all the times that you pull a fast one on me, eh?

GALAHAD: You see how you have a bad mind? I want to take one of you sitting in the armchair... yes, that's it... to remind me of all the old days.

MOSES: I don't believe you, but it ain't costing nothing... You got flash?

GALAHAD: No man, I forget to bring one. But pull the chair over by the window... it got some sun there... [*They shift the armchair*]... Good. Just sit down, let me see what the light like.

MOSES: Ah! This chair really seen some hard days with me, you know. Maybe I shouldn't sell after all.

GALAHAD: Just hold it like that, Moses... Give us one of them mournful smiles you got... That's it... Hold it! [*Clicks the camera*]

MOSES: I could charge for the picture too!

GALAHAD: Just turn your head the other way, let me take another to make sure... Hold it... [*Camera clicks*].

MOSES: How about giving me a hand to take some things to the basement?

GALAHAD: I really got to rush, boy. Old Joseph want me back on the shop... But you could give me a hand to take the armchair out?

MOSES: I thought you would catch me with something before you leave! All right... [*They lift the armchair and take it out of the door.*]

A few days later, on the pavement near Joseph's shop on Portobello Road. Galahad is about to auction Moses's armchair. There is a small crowd, which includes Cap and Harris and Tolroy who have been asked by Galahad to attend...

TOLROY: I telling you and Cap, Harris, that it is only because Tanty get involve in this business why I come. And I begging you both to hold me back when Galahad appear, otherwise it would be murder here today!

HARRIS: As I understand it, Tolroy, it appears that Galahad has changed his ways and is now trying to make amends for all the trouble he has caused in the past.

TOLROY: You call it trouble? More like havoc and destruction!

CAP: Well boy, what I say is just wait and let's see what he is up to. I got my notebook here, and if I see any signs of discrimination, I will report it to the committee.

HARRIS: I observe there is a large photograph of Tanty in the shop window, apparently dealing with some of Mr. Joseph's customers.

TOLROY: I don't know all the ins and outs of this business yet. All she tell me is that it is a scheme to help Moses pay his passage.

HARRIS: A laudable gesture, I should say.

CAP: No doubt, as long as they don't start to make a collection... But look, Galahad coming...

Galahad comes out with the armchair, which he places on the pavement...

GALAHAD: Ladies and gentlemen, I will be brief, You all know when things boil right down, it ain't have nobody in the world like we West Indians who stand by one another in time of need. And this is a time of need if ever there was one. I notice among you a few friends of Mr. Moses Aloetta, a fellow countryman who has been trying for years to get back to Trinidad, but has never been able to raise sufficient funds. It is in this respect that our proprietor, Mr. Joseph, has kindly offered to come to the rescue. As some of you may know, we already have a sale going on, at cut prices, and each little thing you buy helps to swell the funds to take our countryman back home...

TOLROY: [*Aside*] Listen to the bastard trying to sweet-talk the people!

HARRIS: I must say his eloquence surprises me, though his grammar is atrocious!

CAP: Quiet boy, I am taking notes...

GALAHAD: ...and now I come to this armchair, which look just like an ordinary one, but which rested Moses's weary bones on many a time, and in the deep cold of winter it was a place of sleep for many of his friends. Perhaps one of them that I see in the crowd might like to start the bidding. And remember! Every cent that you spend will speed Moses on his way to the sun, through the generosity of our good host and proprietor, Mr. Joseph, who is always willing to cut prices... What am I bid for this famous armchair, Mr. Harris, that you sit down in so many times?

HARRIS: [*Low voice*] Did he call my name?

TOLROY: Yes, start the bidding quick, let me see what Mr. Galahad up to...

HARRIS: [*Loud voice*] ... Er ... ten bob?

GALAHAD: Ten pounds, you said, Mr. Harris?

HARRIS: [*Quickly*] No no! Ten bob... just a start, old chap.

GALAHAD: Well we got to start somewhere! ... I see Mr. Tolroy there with you... in his conductor's uniform too! Took time off work to attend, eh? What do you think of that, ladies and gentlemen, for friendliness and patriotism?

CROWD VOICE: 'Tain't worth more than twelve bob, that chair!

GALAHAD: Ah! Twelve bob! ...Now that we have had our fun, perhaps Mr. Tolroy would get serious?

TOLROY: If it is for Moses, I will say a pound. But I want to have a talk with you afterwards...

GALAHAD: A pound! That is generous! I better let you all know that Mr. Joseph himself paid ten pounds for this chair, to help the cause! There is free delivery, by special van too! How about you, Cap?

CAP: Me, boy?

GALAHAD: Yes, oh!

CAP: I can get the committee for the freedom of coloured people in Great Britain to give twelve pounds, oh... If I get some notes from Mr. Joseph?

GALAHAD: Twelve pounds! Why Moses has only reached the boat-train in Charing Cross with that. Listen friends, in time to come, this chair will be famous! It is the first time that such an event has taken place in Londontown! I observe an American gentleman there who has been standing bashfully behind the rest of you... Come forward, sir. It is men like you who disprove all the propaganda we hear, about the troubles of our brothers in America! Would you like to examine the chair, sir? I can give you the history of every little tea stain, every little spot...

AMERICAN: That won't be necessary... How about thirty-five bucks?

There is a brief pause as Galahad considers this. Meantime, one woman in the crowd to another...

WEST INDIAN WOMAN: Come on, Hannah! This shop always having a sale! Let's go get the pigfoot before they sell out!

The crowd starts to drift off, leaving only Moses's friends and the American.

GALAHAD: [*In a low voice as the American examines the chair*] Thirty-five pounds, you said, sir?

AMERICAN: That's a lot of money, John... Unless it's got some historic value? Where'd you get it from?

GALAHAD: I can't rightly remember at the moment... I believe it originally came from Windsor Castle, but I could be wrong...

AMERICAN: H'mm... I said bucks, not pounds. Tell you what, though. I'm picking up some curios on my trip, and maybe I could give the folks back home a laugh with this chair.

GALAHAD: They would laugh till their belly burst, sir! I'm sure.

AMERICAN: I'll give you fifty bucks, and count yourself lucky.

GALAHAD: Sold! Where you want it deliver, sir? You want me to send it to the ship... [*Laughs*] I mean, airport?...

Back at Moses's room. He is narrating...

MOSES: Of course, I didn't know nothing about all this. In fact, I was sitting down moping in the basement room, because I was still a long way from my passage money, when I hear a knock at the door. I was *mad* not to open it, thinking it was a visit from one of my enemies. And when I did open the door, I didn't see one enemy, but the whole lot of them...

He opens the door, to be faced by Tanty, Bob, Galahad, Tolroy, Cap and Harris. They are loaded with drinks and food...

MOSES: Lord! What the set of you doing here?

HARRIS: Perhaps I better get in front, Tanty, and explain the whole thing to my good friend?

TANTY: [*Snappily*] Keep quiet! If anybody go in first, it's Bob. Come on, Bob, you've been the best friend he had, don't mind you white!

MOSES: Bob! What's happening tonight?

TANTY: [*In a low voice to Bob*] Make the speech that I tell you about!

BOB: Well! Er... Bart and Big City send their best regards, and regret they are unable to attend, but...

TANTY: Oh keep quiet, Bob! Let me do it! ...Moses, ain't you going to let us in?

MOSES: [*Bewildered*] Sure... sure... Don't know where you all going to sit and stand, though...

They troop into the basement room. One of them soon starts opening the bottles and laying out the food. Tanty explains to Moses...

TANTY: Now Moses. What happen was this, you see. I get everybody feeling guilty about the way they treat you, and I went and get a job, and... we come here to present you with a cheque for fifty pounds, which I will explain...

The sound of a record drowns out Tanty's explanation. Later, as the party is in full swing, Moses is still dazed, and can't believe his good luck...

MOSES: Galahad, I still don't see how you manage to get the money off Mr. Joseph.

GALAHAD: I threaten him. I say I would expose all the rackets he carry on to the police...

CAP: Don't forget me, boy! I say I would report him to the committee and set him up as an example of discrimination to the coloured community.

TANTY: [*Sarcastic*] And of course, I didn't do anything, except, if it wasn't for me, this wouldn't have happened! Me, and Bob.

MOSES: How did Bob get into it?

BOB: Bob was the chief adviser. He is the one who tell Galahad to threaten Joseph when he didn't want to give the money!

MOSES: That left you, Harris, and Tolroy?

HARRIS: Well, for my part, old chap, I kept law and order throughout the proceedings. You know how these people get out of hand as soon as they get an idea. Actually, I was the one who besought Bob's assistance...

MOSES: I wouldn't bother to ask Tolroy, because he never done me wrong.

TOLROY: I attend all the discussions about what we plan, Moses. I must of lost a few day's pay!

MOSES: And my absent friends? Bart and Big City?

TANTY: Bart give two pounds. He said he would of made it two pounds ten, but he needed the ten shillings badly! And Big City say he would save you fares, and drive you straight to the ship, or the airport, whenever you ready to leave for Trinidad! Lucky he got a big long-distance van, because all your friends coming to see you off!

MOSES: Well, well! It look as if I made it at last! What you think, Bob? This cheque from Mr. Joseph might bounce!

BOB: No fears! That would get him into some real trouble, which I'm sure he doesn't want.

GALAHAD: Now listen, Moses. It have certain things I want you to do for me when you get back home...

TANTY: That remind me! As you going to be passing Jamaica, Moses, I wonder if you would mind looking up a good friend in Kingston. It not out of your way...

HARRIS: Old chap, my business is more important. When you get back to Trinidad, I want you to...

CAP: Boy, oh? We got to think of spreading out the black races, you know, the way how things going in Brit'n. I want you to check

134

if it have any immigrants from Nigeria who reside in Trinidad. Ask them if they have any colour problems...

Moses is back in the present talking to the reporter.

MOSES: ...So there you are. I give you the whole story.

REPORTER: So at last you're going! When do you leave?

MOSES: I got a passage fix for tomorrow, and Big City bringing the van to collect my things, and my friends, and take us to Plymouth, where the ship leaving from.

REPORTER: Well, I do wish you well.

MOSES: One thing, though. I ain't covered for incidental expenses nor that little capital which may set me going in Trinidad.

REPORTER: What do you mean, Moses?

MOSES: [*Chuckling*] You didn't think I was talking all this time for nothing, did you? I got some capital to get from your newspaper, ain't I?

REPORTER: But of course! I forgot about that! I have a cheque here for you...

MOSES: Well just lead me to the cash office, and that will set me up for a while. Mind you, I not promising not to return to Brit'n, in which case, maybe I could give you another interview, telling you how the situation is down there in Trinidad...

The End

James C. Aboud	*Lagahoo Poems*	£7.99
Kevyn Alan Arthur	*The View from Belmont*	£8.99
Laurence A. Breiner	*Black Yeats*	£16.99
Mark De Brito	*Heron's Canoe*	£7.99
Brenda Flanagan	*You Alone are Dancing*	£7.99
Anson Gonzalez	*Crossroads of Dream*	£7.99
Anson Gonzalez	*Collected Poems*	£8.99
Vishnu Gosine	*The Coming of Lights*	£7.99
Cecil Gray	*The Woolgatherer*	£8.99
Ismith Khan	*The Crucifixion*	£7.99
Ismith Khan	*A Day in the Country*	£8.99
Rabindranath Maharaj	*The Writer and his Wife*	£8.99
L. Manoo-Rahming	*Curry Flavour*	£7.99
marina maxwell	*Decades to Ama*	£9.99
marina maxwell	*Chopstix in Mauby*	£8.99
Sharlow Mohammed	*The Elect*	£7.99
Lakshmi Persaud	*Sastra*	£9.99
Lakshmi Persaud	*Butterfly In The Wind*	£7.99
Jennifer Rahim	*Between The Fence And The Forest*	£7.99
Jennifer Rahim	*Songster and Other Stories*	£8.99
Raymond Ramcharitar	*American Fall*	£7.99
Eric Merton Roach	*The Flowering Rock*	£9.99
Sam Selvon	*Highway in the Sun*	£8.99
Sam Selvon	*Eldorado West One*	£7.99
Martin Zehnder	*Something Rich and Strange*: *Selected Essays on Samuel Selvon*	£14.99

JENNIFER RAHIM
Songster and Other Stories

Rahim's stories move between the present and the past to make sense of the tensions between image and reality in contemporary Trinidad. The contemporary stories show the traditional, communal world in retreat before the forces of local and global capitalism. A popular local fisherman is gunned down when he challenges the closure of the beach for a private club catering to white visitors and the new elite; the internet becomes a rare safe place for an AIDS sufferer to articulate her pain; cocaine has become the scourge even of the rural communities. But the stories set thirty years earlier in the narrating 'I's' childhood reveal that the 'old-time' Trinidad was already breaking up. The old pieties about nature symbolised by belief in the presence of the folk-figure of 'Papa Bois' are powerless to prevent the ruthless plunder of the forests; communal stability has already been uprooted by the pulls towards emigration, and any sense that Trinidad was ever edenic is undermined by images of the destructive power of alcohol and the casual presence of paedophilic sexual abuse.

Rahim's Trinidad, is though, as her final story makes clear, the creation of a writer who has chosen to stay, and she is highly conscious that her perspective is very different from those who have taken home away in a suitcase, or who visit once a year. Her Trinidad is 'not a world in my head like a fantasy', but the island that 'lives and moves in the bloodstream'. Her reflection on the nature of small island life is as fierce and perceptive as Jamaica Kincaid's *A Small Place*, but comes from and arrives at a quite opposite place. What Rahim finds in her island is a certain existential insouciance and the capacity of its people, whatever their material circumstance, to commit to life in the knowledge of its bitter-sweetness.

ISBN 13:9781845230487
UKList price: £8.99 US$19.95 CAN$24.95

NEW 2007

LAURENCE A. BREINER
Black Yeats: Eric Roach and the Politics of Caribbean Poetry

For readers of West Indian literature, a study of Eric Roach requires no justification. He is the most significant poet in the English-speaking Caribbean between Claude McKay (who spent nearly all of his life abroad) and Derek Walcott. Roach began publishing in the late 1930s and continued, with a few interruptions, until 1974, the year of his suicide. His career thus spans an extraordinary period of Anglophone Caribbean history, from the era of violent strikes that led to the formation of most of the region's political parties, through the process of decolonization, the founding and subsequent failure of the Federation of the West Indies (1958-1962), and the coming of Independence in the 1960s. This book presents a critical analysis of all of Roach's published poetry, but it presents that interpretation as part of a broader study of the relations between his poetic activity, the political events he experienced (especially West Indian Federation, Independence, the Black Power movement, the "February Revolution" of 1970 Trinidad), and the seminal debates about art and culture in which he participated.

By exploring Roach's work within its conditions, this book aims above all to confirm Roach's rightful place among West Indian and metropolitan poets of comparable gifts and accomplishments.

Laurence Breiner is the author of the critically acclaimed *Introduction to West Indian Poetry*.

ISBN 13:9781845230470
UK List Price: £17.99 US$34.95 CAN$43.95

NEW 2007

TRINIDADIAN WRITERS FROM PEEPAL TREE PRESS

James Christopher Aboud
Kevin Baldeosingh
Faustin Charles
Mark De Brito
Brenda Flanagan
Anson Gonzalez
Vishnu Gosine
Cecil Gray
Ismith Khan
Rabindranath Maharaj
Lelawatee Manoo-Rahming
marina ama omowale maxwell
Ian McDonald
Sharlow Mohammed
Lakshmi Persaud
Jennifer Rahim
Raymond Ramcharitar
Eric Merton Roach
Sam Selvon

Peepal Tree Press is celebrated as the home of
challenging and inspiring literature from the Caribbean
and Black Britain. We publish fiction, poetry, literary
criticism, memoirs and historical studies.

www.peepaltreepress.com

Peepal Tree Press, 17 King's Avenue, Leeds LS6 1QS, UK
Tel: +44 (0) 113 2451703
E-mail: contact@peepaltreepress.com